No Soap, Less School

No Soap, Less School

Ron Bridge

First published in Great Britain in 2019 by
Chillies Oast Publishing.

Edited, designed and produced by Tandem Publishing Limited
http://tandempublishing.yolasite.com/

ISBN: 978-1-5272-4578-5

10 9 8 7 6 5 4 3 2 1

A CIP catalogue record for this book is available from the
British Library.

Printed and bound in Great Britain by CPI Group (UK) Ltd,
Croydon CR0 4YY.

I dedicate this book to my wife Sue for putting up with me for sixty years...

... and to our eldest son Adrian for arranging the printing.

Bridge Family, 1905. Albert Henry, Granny,
Jessie, Freda, Harold and Leo.

Contents

Preface

This is the true story of an English boy caught up by war and then civil war in China. As I write, seventy-five years later, despite the time lapse I find I have never really forgotten the events of those days. Yet, although always remembering vividly what happened, I did not let those memories interfere with what became a very full career, and indeed would seldom voluntarily mention the experience to anyone. Then, about thirty years ago, our four children virtually sat on me and said, 'Dad, you must talk, you are history!'

Even so, I procrastinated for another quarter of a century, not thinking it worthwhile. Then one day, looking in an old suitcase, I came across a piece of parachute silk, long thought lost; written on the silk were the pencilled names of seven US military personnel. I also found my late mother's diaries, which included the names of those same seven individuals. The majority of her diaries had been written during the Second World War, on odd scraps of semi-transparent air-mail paper, both sides covered in pencil and margins full of even more writing. These documents confirmed my recollections and also furnished the precise dates of key events, whereas my own memories had parameters defined, for example, by such vagaries as '… early in the second year…' or '… the summer of the last year…' This information has now enabled me to really tell my story, which concerns living in a foreign country, enduring the privations of a Japanese prison camp during the Second World War, and then being caught up in the midst of a civil war in the Far East.

My wife has been an author and writer for over forty years and her encouragement provided the final impetus in my putting pen to paper. Weihsien Camp in China's Shandong Province is a place of which some readers may have heard: Eric Liddell, the missionary teacher and 1924 Olympic gold medallist, immortalised in the film *Chariots of Fire*, died in February 1945 whilst interned there. I was nine years old when I entered that camp, where I was to spend over two and a half years as a 'guest' of the Japanese Emperor. But that is only part of the story. The tale then moves on to Tianjin, a city of two million at the time of which I write. Although not one of the original treaty ports, as agreed between China and Britain in the last half of the 19th century as reparations after the 'Opium Wars', Tianjin mushroomed enormously after it achieved that status, which it held for over eighty years (1858 until 1944). It has now swelled to 12 million and its factories and warehouses spread to the coast at Dagu. But then it was home.

Whilst this is my story, I have included background facts of life immediately before, at the time, and up to near the end of the Korean War. Life was so different to what it is now as I write, in the first quarter of the 21st century. I hope I do not offend by using what may now be considered politically incorrect words or phrases, but the term 'politically correct' had not even entered into English vocabulary in the 1930s to 1950s, the timeframe of this book, and I write as I have recalled matters, describing them in the idiom and usage of contemporary English. I hope that the additional background information will give some clarity and understanding to the reader.

As for my children, who urged me to write this memoir, I must apologise to them, and to my ten grandchildren, that I did not tell them in person some of the details of this convoluted story.

—Ronald William 'Ron' Bridge MBE AFC FRAeS FRIN, Sussex, February 2019

Tientsin (Tianjin) and its surroundings.

1

Enter Ron

A frequent question that I have had to answer during my life has been: 'Why were you living in China?' Thus a few words of explanation as to how and why the Bridge family found themselves in North China during the latter years of Queen Victoria's and then King Edward VII's reign, and so were 'caught' by the Japanese in 1941 and detained until 1945. Then, post-Second World War, how and why the family stayed beyond 1945, with the hope that trade and life would return to the standards of the 1920s and 1930s, a dream comprehensively shattered by the Chinese civil war.

In the latter part of the 19th century, the expansion of British interests had taken many guises; the British Empire increased its territories and political domination was paramount. To achieve that aim the apparent emphasis was on trade first of all, but the authorities also felt that forcing the spread of Christianity would assist the imperial project. Britain, through its Indian-based East India Company (EIC), had been thwarted in these aims by China, which considered itself, at that time and maybe even today, the centre of the universe. The EIC had traded to and from the south-east coast of China since the early 17th century, by taking China tea to the British Isles and paying for it by exporting Benares opium to China, grown and processed in India. The Chinese Emperors wanted to bring a halt to the opium trade, although British commercial interests wished to keep it, as it was very lucrative, and had been largely fostered by the British Government via the East India Company since the early 17th century. This policy difference culminated in the 'Opium Wars' of the 1840s, and the subsequent peace treaties that ultimately granted to Britain the colony of Hong Kong 'in perpetuity'. The settlements also gave Britain the right to have and govern enclaves known as 'Treaty Ports' within selected Chinese cities.

Tianjin[1] had not one been among the original Treaty Ports,[2] negotiated at the Treaty of Nanking (1842), which had concentrated on the south of China,[3] where trading access had been granted already for a number of years, and which was known to ships' masters and traders alike. Post the 1842 Treaty there was a troubled truce, and it became evident that to really influence policy Britain needed to have convenient contact with China's capital, as the overland journeys over near-unpaved roads were not practicable.

In the 19th century sea travel was the only logical means of intercontinental travel, and Tianjin, some thirty miles up the Hai Ho (Hai River) from its mouth at Daku,[4] was effectively the gateway to Beijing.[5] The capital lay some eighty miles north-west of the river mouth, but the narrow and shallow river mouth meant that ships with a draught in excess of 14 feet (4 metres)[6] could not proceed up-river, but it was nevertheless an essential means of communication to the capital, and the only sensible one. Tianjin lay at the confluence of the Grand Canal and the Hai Ho, and up until 1782 had been a Chinese military station.[7] Since Britain, France and America were demanding revision to the treaties due to commercial and ecclesiastical pressure, a further war broke out between Britain and China. This was terminated by the 1858 Treaty of Tianjin[8] (then spelt Tientsin, by foreigners), which among other concessions granted the right of travel to the interior by foreigners and the right of freedom of faith for Christians and a dramatic increase in the number of Treaty Ports. It had been found that the early Treaty Ports along the south-east coast were of limited value, as communication from the hinterland was difficult due to the coastal hills. Shanghai, Tianjin, and Canton, with their rivers leading into the heart of China, became ever more practicable. The opium trade had virtually ceased, but a vast catalogue of other goods became available, creating a lucrative import and export trade with China.

Ultimately, in quantity of trade and importance, Tianjin was propelled into prominence, second only to Shanghai and the only other place where the British Army was permanently stationed within China proper. Hong Kong and the new territories were Crown colonies, and for the first twenty years after China opened up were administered differently, through the Colonial Office in London, whereas China remained in the domain of the Foreign Office. Even so, up until the end of the Second World War, Hong Kong was of less importance to Great Britain than Shanghai in both quantity of trade and political influence.

The London Missionary Society had been represented in China since 1807, when Robert Morrison arrived, but growth and hence missionary activity had been inhibited due to the restrictions on inland travel placed by Chinese officialdom and the sheer difficulty of travel, at best by mule cart or on the rivers in sampans. It was not until after the 1858 Treaty of Tianjin that any meaningful expansion of British, European and American Missions could take place, and they were responsible for China's initial exposure to foreign education and Western medicine. As far as Britain was concerned, the exploitation of the newly negotiated possibilities was slow to take effect, partly due to a severe shortage of personnel; a massive recruitment drive was needed in the British Isles for service in China. The appetite was there, though, with the awakening Chinese population relentless in its pursuit of education. In 1865 Hudson Taylor founded the China Inland Mission (CIM) in England as a non-denominational Christian Protestant Mission, and the CIM decided in 1885 to send the first hundred missionaries from the British Isles to China to preach.

Albert Henry Bridge, my paternal grandfather, had been born in Glamorgan in 1868. His father, John Bridge, an Anglican, had come to the county from Lancashire to take up a position as a mining engineer in the South Wales coalfield. John died of pneumonia when his son was four and my great-grandmother re-married four years later. Albert Henry's stepfather, George Palmer,[9] was a miner as well; but also a Methodist lay preacher, and he had a great influence on the young Albert Henry. Albert started work in the Welsh coal mines at age twelve, but he spent his evenings walking four miles into Pontypridd to get an education. Licensed by the non-Conformists to preach by the age of fifteen, he gave up work and enrolled full-time at Pontypridd Academy to become a Methodist Minister. The China Inland Mission recruiting drive interested him and he walked to London from Pontypridd in 1886 and was accepted by the Rev. Hudson Taylor, sailing from Tilbury on 1st December 1887 on the SS *Brindisi*.[10] Arriving in Shanghai in January 1888 A. H. Bridge was sent immediately to the language school at Anqing, and just over a year later was working amongst opium addicts in Henan Province.

Then, in early 1891 a site at Weichen near the Grand Canal[11] was found; it was also not far from the junction of the Grand Canal and the Hai River, and at that time near the course of the Yellow River. A. H. Bridge was sent there, where he founded a mission.[12] Strong-willed, he resigned from the CIM in 1893 but retained the Weichen property and continued as an independent missionary. Returning to England in 1896, he married Minnie Trick the next year in Bristol; she had also been in China as the governess to a missionary family, and after the birth of their first daughter, Constance Freda, the Bridges returned to China in 1898.

Albert Henry then joined the London Missionary Society, bringing with him the Weichen Mission property, but as he was not ordained it was a turbulent relationship[13] in which the LMS sought to put him on a lower pay scale, which culminated in his resignation in 1909.[14] He retained the ownership of the property, having 'employed' a Mr MacFarlane to oversee matters ecclesiastical, and a series of medical experts to oversee the other aspects of a mission. He always maintained his language skills, and ultimately joined the Chinese Salt Administration, which enforced an Imperial monopoly. During this time he had had to escape the Boxer Rebellion with his wife and two daughters, initially by cart to the Shandong coast and then by sailing junk[15] to Yantai[16] before boarding a steamer to Kobe, Japan. From where he volunteered as an interpreter for the Allied forces employed in the Relief of Beijing, and was sent to Tianjin.

After the Boxer insurrection ended Albert Henry was active for the next two years in travelling round the country, restoring relations between Chinese and foreigners. The Chinese appreciated his efforts, and the Emperor, who was dictated to by Cixi or the 'Empress Dowager',[17] granted Royal Letters Patent bestowing the rank of Mandarin of the 4th order, the formal presentation being made by the Viceroy Yuan Shikai in January 1903.[18] With this grant of the rank he was given a piece of land near the seashore at Beidaihe (then spelt Petaiho) of 300 mu (50 acres) on which he built a bungalow and stable blocks in 1904. He further built a two-storey house and a small two-bedroom bungalow in 1924. By 1930 he had reduced his property somewhat, selling a parcel of land to other Britons who wanted a house by the sea.

Although his language skills were of necessary value to British officialdom and British entrepreneurs alike, Albert Henry would not have been totally accepted by them despite having a daughter who married a Consul. For, in keeping with all who were or had been missionaries, he wore classic Chinese clothes whilst trying to convert Chinese to Christianity and whilst living away from the Treaty Ports. Colonial mores frowned on 'going native'.

He kept the Weichen property and endowed it, employing a missionary and a doctor, where it flourished as a mission and medical treatment centre until it was deliberately burnt down by the advancing Japanese Army in 1937, destroying his extensive collection of Chinese books and the recorded tomes of research he had been doing, mainly to graft European-type fruit trees on to Chinese root stock, as well as the trees themselves. He, primarily, was very much a sinologist and language expert, being fluent in seven dialects[19] of Chinese and the national language, now known as Mandarin. Increasingly, from 1909, he had stayed in Tianjin or in the property at Beidaihe. To us grandchildren, he seemed a disciplinarian, yet was always willing to impart knowledge, especially on Chinese language and agriculture. The youngest of his four children, Albert Lionel 'Leo' (born in 1904 at Weichen), was my father, who initially attended the British-run 'Grammar' school in Tianjin.

The First World War prevented my father from making the journey to England for education there from the age of thirteen, as was the destiny of most of his contemporaries living in the Far East. As soon as it was possible, my father was sent to finish off school in 1919 at Abbotsholme, Derbyshire, when he was fifteen, returning to Tianjin in 1923. There my father joined Harold, his elder brother, in a local British firm, Pottinger & Co., that had been founded in the 1880s, importing flour, and machine tools, exporting wool, frozen eggs and bean curd, and managing property mainly within the British Concession, where *de facto* British title to land had been granted. Pottinger & Co. also managed Knowles & Co., which concentrated on import and export, and the Hotung Land Co. Ltd, which concentrated on property.

Leo married Margot Fleet in All Saints Anglican Church, Tianjin on 24th September 1932, with a guard of honour of the British Boy Scouts, of whom he was the Scoutmaster. He was later to become assistant Scout Commissioner for North China and was awarded the Scout's Order of Merit by Baden-Powell. His wife had been born in Dewsbury, Yorkshire; her father, Herbert Alexander Fleet, was an electrical engineer specialising in building and installing power stations. Margot's early childhood was spent living in Dewsbury and then Wimbledon, while her father worked on London Electricity power stations such as Lots Road.

Part of the spin-off from the opening up of China was the identified need to modernise, and this was readily apparent at the Tongshan coal mines north-east of Beijing. They had been worked for nearly a century at a human cost that no one can ever really estimate; the importance of the industry was recognised by the construction of Mieshan (a man-made coal hill) which was situated adjacent to the Palace in the Imperial City. The British Government saw the mines as a potential and convenient source of fuel for the Royal Navy's Pacific Fleet and for the factories of India. As a result they recruited my maternal grandfather to electrify the Mines, run by the Kailan Mining Administration. At the end of his contract he elected to stay on in Tianjin as a private consultant electrical engineer and marine surveyor for Lloyd's of London. His wife Elizabeth Everson Fleet had accompanied her husband to China, travelling with their daughter Margot across the Trans-Siberian Railway in 1913. They were returning to England by the same route from the first China contract when they were delayed in St Petersburg due to the 1917 Russian Revolution.

A year later they travelled back to China the same way. Living in Tongshan initially, they moved to Tianjin in 1924 where Mum finished her education at the sixth form of the Tientsin Grammar School in the British Concession.

2

Growing Up

By 1934, when I arrived on the scene, Tianjin's British Concession was probably in its heyday; but it was a society which, if analysed, remained artificial in concept, and liable to rapid change from external pressure. But no one wished to think about that, let alone talk of it. There had been a few troubles in mid-China on the Yangtze River in 1927–8, a thousand miles to the south, and there were always warlords floating around the countryside with their private armies. However, no one dared offend the British or touch anything British: the Union Jack was sacrosanct. Yet although an Anglo-Japanese Alliance had been signed in 1922, Japan detected that Britain's wealth had taken such a battering during the First World War that its influence would surely decline, and although Japan had been allied to the Western powers from the time of the Boxer Rebellion through to the end of the First World War, Japan saw an opening to expand its influence. The goal was to replace the perceived waning influence of the British Empire with a 'South-East Asia Co-prosperity Sphere'. But it had not yet happened, and Japan had realised it would not happen unless it could control the governments of the region.

Events were still riding on the enormous steamroller

started by Britain's East India Company. The Royal Navy was still the largest navy in the world and Britain's merchant fleet carried the world's trade. The latter had developed Shanghai into a major seaport, where lived a selection of people drawn from all strata of British society, from tramps to taipans.[20] Only coastal ships, usually of 3–4,000 tons, could get up to Tianjin; they had British officers but used Chinese seamen. They carried deck passengers who were segregated from the cabins and the working part of the ship by iron grills, barbed wire and guards, to prevent a take-over of the ship by the ever-present pirates who operated along the China coast. Those anti-pirate guards were generally ex-Indian Army personnel, Ghurkhas or Sikhs, armed with .303 rifles.

The British community numbered about a thousand strong in Tianjin, and was made up of teachers, managers and administrators, mainly products of the English public school system, which had expanded in Queen Victoria's reign to meet the 'upsurge of industrial growth and of British prestige throughout the world'.[21] There was a resident British Army Battalion, a Royal Navy Ship in the river port and a British-officered police force, with NCOs recruited from the Russian Community[22] and constables from the south of China. British missionaries also abounded, but their penchant for wearing Chinese clothes and mixing with the Chinese working man meant little social contact with the business community, and the missionary abhorrence of gambling meant that they did not frequent the racecourse. To put it bluntly, missionaries were another breed: recognised by the British Consular authorities as British, but the wider British community accepted them only on sufferance.

The 'British Concession' in Tianjin was protected by the resident British Army battalion (in 1934 the 1st Bn Queen's

Regiment), and the Royal Navy generally had a sloop moored on the river's Bund.[23] The Tianjin Club flourished, where Dad would spend time drinking a social pre-lunch gin and tonic or sometimes a cold Ewo or Quingdao beer. Located in the centre of the business district of the British Concession, the Club's membership was confined to British businessmen, with Americans accepted reluctantly. Other nationalities could be invited as guests, although members of the Asian communities were positively discouraged and the only Chinese allowed were the Club's own staff.

Across 'Victoria Park' the British Concession was governed from a magnificent pseudo-castle, Gordon Hall, built fifty years previously in honour of 'Chinese' Gordon of the Taiping rebellion and Khartoum fame. In the Victoria grounds stood a three-quarter-sized replica of the Cenotaph in Whitehall, erected in 1923 on the site of the 'Bell', which had been moved from the old walled Chinese city when the walls had been demolished in 1860 by the British Army. Across the road stood the Astor House Hotel, which had housed visitors and travellers alike for the previous thirty or more years.

The Country Club on the south-west corner of the British Concession allowed women as members; they had to have an alternate venue to their houses to play bridge and mah-jong![24] The Country Club boasted a full-sized swimming pool and its grounds had a golf course, sailing and rowing lakes, as well as an ornamental lake, which doubled for skating in the winter when frozen over. Membership again was restricted to the British, with similar rules as applied to the main Club.

As far as the British went, marriage to other European nationalities was tolerated, but not to Russians. A British male showing any such inclinations was first talked to by his superiors and then, if necessary, quietly transferred to another city, a fate that happened to many members of the foreign-officered China Maritime Customs, who were often outside the pale of the Tianjin Club. If the offender did persist he was black-balled from the Club, and effectively became a non-person, as did anyone who married a Chinese, when it was immediately and quietly suggested that they seek employment and accommodation in some other city or Concession preferably not under British Administration. Normally a French Concession, where the rules were more tolerant, or the defunct Belgian, German or Russian Concessions, which were nominally managed by the Chinese, but effectively 'just ran themselves'.

The British Concession had three open spaces within its boundaries. Victoria Park to the south of the Gordon Hall, with a bandstand and flower gardens. The Recreation Ground, which was an open city block next to the Union Church and within a few blocks of the Bund; it had a pavilion on its west side. Lastly there was the Minyuan Ground, again an open city block surrounded by housing and apartments. The one British-managed recreation area that tolerated all non-Chinese nationalities was the Race Club, where money could be made by the Club for its debenture holders from the Tote. China ponies were raced on the flat, with the British debenture holders in their luxurious stand, another stand for other nationalities and the Chinese milling round the ground off the track. In the spring, point-to-point racing was held to the east of the Concessions, near to where the airport would be built. Both the sites were always complete with Chinese 'bookies' as the Chinese are, by nature, great gamblers.

The British Concession was part of Britain, and:

Land of Hope and Glory, Mother of the Free,
How shall we extol thee, who are born of thee?
Wider still and wider shall thy bounds be set;
God, who made thee mighty, Make thee mightier yet,

was rammed down my and every Anglo-Saxon British child's throat, loud and clear enough to rub off on other nationalities, who often unwittingly hummed the tune.

Everything was based on or mirrored England, including the Tianjin Grammar School, run and administered by Englishmen and based on the British educational system. The majority of the Anglo-Saxon British children used the Grammar School as a feeder for the years of 'going home [i.e. England] to school'; the other British used it as a copy of the public schools they could never aspire to, and it served other nationalities who were to be inculcated into the British way of thinking. The standard curriculum, with examinations leading to Cambridge University's school certificate, which were held each December, was used in all schools. The pupils of the Tianjin Grammar School, British and foreign alike, started the day with prayers from the *Book of Common Prayer* and sang Hymns from *Ancient and Modern*, the school song was 'Forty Years On', so drummed into me, time and time again, that seventy-five years later I can still remember the words.

Forty Years on, when afar and asunder
Parted are those who are singing today,
When you look back and forgetfully wonder
What you were like in your work and your play—
Then, it may be, there will often come o'er you,
Glimpse of notes like the catch of a song—

Visions of boyhood shall float them before you,
Echoes of dreamland shall bear them along.
Follow up! Follow up! Follow up! Follow up! Follow up!
Till the field ring again and again
With the tramp of the twenty-two men—
Follow up! Follow up!

Chinese students at mission schools run for Chinese children followed the same curriculum. This was guided by a principle unchanged for nearly a century: give these boys (girls were always an afterthought) a solid education in their language and in ours – English. Instruct them in the British system and bind them by a link that could not easily be severed.[25] American mission schools taught an American curriculum and other countries generally applied a similar philosophy. The Chinese realised that the only universally recognised datum of achievement was English and the Cambridge Overseas School Certificate, thus, due to demand, a curriculum based on achieving that aim was increasingly adopted in French, Irish, Dutch and German-run Roman Catholic Mission schools, as well as the Protestant mission schools, although these latter were few and far between.

The British Concession's calendar always called for an annual sports day, held on the Recreation Ground on Empire Day (24th May), for a military parade on the King's Birthday (usually the first Saturday in June) and on Remembrance Day (11th November). Poppies were on sale in aid of the Royal British Legion, and a parade centred on the Cenotaph on Victoria Road.

Japan had first invaded China in 1931, but the Sino-Japanese War proper did not really break out until July 1937, with an incident in Beijing.[26] Japanese and Chinese military were camped near the Marco Polo Bridge there.

Small-arms fire was exchanged, which got out of hand and war was declared. A huge Union Flag was painted on the tarmac of the Minyuan Ground, and was largely respected by the Japanese pilots when strafing Tianjin. This caused a large number of influential Chinese to buy houses in 1938 overlooking the Minyuan, because they valued the protection of the Union Jack.

The British Consul-General, who doubled as the Judge of the British Court, tried cases under British law and was subservient to the British Supreme Court for the Far East in Shanghai, which in turn reported to the High Court in London, and ultimately the House of Lords. Everything was done to the theme 'we are British and hence must, by definition, set the standard for all other nations to copy. The Concession is part of Britain and Britain itself is "home".'

Britain had split off its Diplomatic Corps and further instituted a China Consular Corps. With the outbreak of war in Europe in 1939 the Concessions across China went into overdrive to support the mother country: ladies knitted for British troops, other ladies tore up bales of calico to wind bandages. Money was raised to buy Spitfires for defence of the homeland.[27] It went without question that I joined the Wolf Cubs of the Scout movement as young as possible to serve, as Baden-Powell had put it, 'King and country'.

I had been brought up in a variation of the norm in the British Community. My parents, both being fluent Mandarin-speakers, as all the servants and staff were, reasoned that I would often be in the company of my amah,[28] and they didn't want to confuse me with other languages. So I only spoke Chinese until the age of four, when English was slipped into the conversation, albeit slowly, and written Chinese would come later (to master written Chinese meant learning about 4,000 characters). This approach was one that my grandfather had used successfully for his four children, all of whom as adults were in Tianjin in 1941.

From 1934 to 1937 I had been taken by my parents to Beidaihe for the entire summer, then returned to Tianjin, while my father used to commute to Beidaihe for the weekends from Tianjin; Funainai,[29] my amah, always came with me. Mum felt that it was pointless employing an amah and doing the work herself. 1938 was different in that, after returning to Tianjin from Beidaihe, we went on another holiday. I suppose in a way it was the start of my global wanderings. My father, mother and I got on a Japanese coastal ship and went off to Japan for three weeks as a change; China and Japan being at war, the amah stayed in Tianjin and went off to see her family.

The ship was a new experience: I spent my time at sea playing deck quoits, and my memory has been refreshed by the 8mm home movies taken by Dad at the time. Japan's Inland Sea seemed to be all about visiting seaside caves by small steam-driven tenders and watching overweight ladies doing exercises on the beach to get their weight down using an idiosyncratic form of yoga. Soon after we got back to Tianjin, Dad had to go up to Beidaihe for the funeral of his father, my grandfather Albert Bridge. Sadly, Albert Henry had not been in good health since the Japanese had burnt down his library and the Weichen buildings. Albert Henry had effectively died of a broken heart.

In early April 1939 the Japanese began being difficult, quarantining the various foreign Concessions in Tianjin. Barriers on the British Concession were manned on the British side by the 1st Battalion Durham Light Infantry. Then the Japanese started trying to ban all British and French exports: this caused grief to the commercial interests and the Royal Navy despatched HMS *Sandwich* from the

RN's base in Hong Kong as a guard-ship, which moored on the Bund opposite our flat. My parents soon befriended the Captain, Cmdr Bayliss RN, and I was able to visit the ship the following year, which was a real treat for a six-year-old.

Mother Nature created a diversion in July 1939 when the Hai Ho River burst its banks and Tianjin was flooded. The deepest floodwater lay in the old city, becoming shallower as it went south, so that around the area of the Tianjin Club it stood about knee-deep, although by the west of the British Concession the water was shoulder-deep. In an attempt to help the Chinese, large numbers of mud 'Igloos' were built on any available dry land to house people fleeing into Tianjin from the surrounding villages; evidence of the flood up-country was daily visible from our flat: drowned bodies, both human and animal, floated down the river. Within the Concessions the hawkers put their products into tin baths and floated them from door to door, whilst the larger items were transported on hastily constructed rafts. Although the water level precluded the use of cars it did not prevent the rickshaw boys plying their trade, and the 'expats' made use of them, although the stench from the near stagnant water, with sewage leaking into it continuously, was almost unbearable.

The floods put paid to my nursery school attendance, where I always remember day one, a year earlier. The school was run by Miss Stuart in the All Saints Church Hall at the junction of Meadows Road and Race Course Road. We were assembled and trying to master the intricacies of knitting and I, seeing that Miss Stuart was briefly out of the room, stood up and announced, 'This is boring, let's go out and play!' Just as everyone thought it was a good idea, Miss Stuart returned, lessons were resumed and I ended up contemplating the corner of the room for most of the rest of the day.

Before the 'floods', Japan had begun putting up knife-rest barbed wire barriers and manning the few entry points with sentries, building tarmac ramps about a foot high to deter vehicles. The object was to hinder or restrict movement in and out of the British Concession. The Japanese Army often conducted strip searches of foreigners, in order to make life difficult. A New Zealand business colleague of my father, Cecil Davis, had the indignity of being stripped and left standing bare while his passport was examined, and he was not alone in being subjected to such treatment. This sparked British annoyance, which rapidly became outrage, particularly when they started trying to do it to the ladies. The Japanese finally succumbed to diplomatic pressure to lift the blockade. Things were really changing, but the British inhabitants of the Concessions agreed that they had seen it all before … and they had.

There was much talk by my parents and their friends about the re-forming of the Tianjin Volunteer Corps, in which my father had served in the 1920s until it had been scrapped by the War Office in London as an 'economy measure'. The financial saving came from the disbanding of two posts: an 'adjutant' and a Sergeant drill instructor. In the end the British authorities realised that Tianjin was impossible to defend, with the 30,000-strong Japanese Army fighting the Chinese Army within thirty miles or so. Thus, in January 1941, regular forces were withdrawn, and the last British Battalion, 2nd East Surrey Regiment,[30] left in March 1941; they had only stayed for a year, having replaced the 1st Durham Light Infantry in 1940.

The Tianjin Municipal Emergency Corps was formed, mostly from the British business community, although a Russian Company was established[31] to give them more of a quasi-police role to counter possible riots. To my eyes,

honed as they were from playing with my 'Britain's Ltd'
toy soldiers, they were inadequately armed, carrying only
0.32 Browning automatics. Anyway, Dad joined them.
Although the 'Russian' company received some remunera-
tion the British businessmen did not; the Russian members
had also retained the Lee-Enfield 0.303 rifles acquired from
the departing East Surreys.[32] The Russians enjoyed further
motivation: serving with British police, or in 'quasi-police'
forces on the China coast, allowed them to apply for a
British passport after only five years' service, rather than the
usual ten years normally required for residency on British
territory before application.

The community would not be panicked; the British would
just call to mind what had happened in 1900, 1915, or
1928 … and carry on. Since the fall of the Chinese Imperial
Family and the 1911 Revolution, which had made Sun Yat-
sen President and in which China had embraced democracy,
warlords of various persuasions had intermittently stirred in
the Chinese countryside, their private armies attempting to
force their will on the populace.

The British business community's attitude, like that of all
other British Concessions in China, was epitomised by a telegram from the British Ambassador to the Foreign Secretary,
Lord Halifax, in Whitehall. 'I do not believe that the mere
renewal of previous warnings will produce any appreciable
result. British community here is case hardened and somewhat embittered by previous evacuation scares…'[33]

The other problem was that non Anglo-Saxon British
passport holders were frowned on by those who were British-
born, or who could trace a direct line of both parents to the
United Kingdom. The dark blue British passport ensured
that they were still the responsibility of His Majesty's
Government, as were the members of what had been 'the

Empire' but was now 'the Commonwealth'. The only safe haven in the Far East, because of the European War, was Australia, and she was enforcing her 'white Australia' policy. Officialdom was aware of the problem '… there is a large Eurasian element here which cannot be ignored in any evacuation scheme and in many cases it is quite impossible to differentiate between any person of "European descent" and others. Consulate registration cards record as being Eurasian, only on occasions when mother is born Chinese.'

One solution would be to send certain arbitrarily selected whites, destitute or otherwise, to Australia and all remainder of the Community to other destinations.[34] This idea faltered when the Australian Government queried who was going to pay for them. In the event, they left 1,500 British passport holders, mainly women and children, in limbo: they were embarked on ships originally intended for Australia but, anchored in Manilla Bay, ended up interned in Manilla by the Japanese. There is a Whitehall Civil Service minute on the files in the United Kingdom National Archives, Kew: 'if there is a war between Britain and Japan surely normal banking will continue and the husbands would, should and could remit money from Japanese occupied territory!' Whitehall has spoken! Yet, without much thought as usual.

There is also a Minute at Kew alluding to a telegram from my Uncle Alwyne Ogden, the Consul at Tianjin, dated Friday 5th December 1941. The telegram had reported that there was a lot of talk in the Chinese bazaars and that the Japanese were planning something on the Monday. It was received at 10 p.m. in Whitehall on Friday night, and the Duty Clerk has scrawled across it: 'Ogden is off on his sleuthing, leave it until Monday.'

Monday was the 8th December and the attack on Pearl Harbor.

3

Recruited by the United Kingdom

A fter the debacle of Dunkirk, and the setbacks in Europe and North Africa, the British Communities in China as in Malaya and the Far East generally realised that they were in for a 'long haul'. Suddenly England became closer, and in response to a plea by Lord Halifax, the UK Foreign Secretary, firms were to remain cohesively functioning in the Far East in support of Britain's war effort, yet also release men to join the British armed forces. What are now known as multinational firms released their younger British employees, and often replaced them with French, Estonians, Danes and Swiss. In the case of local or private companies, one of the partners, generally the junior, would go to 'war'.

My mother was expecting another child in October, which impinged on the discussions between Dad and his elder brother, my Uncle Harold, and the latter decided to leave. In July 1941, he went to join the British Army in the Middle East. When he got to Kolkata[35] he met in a hotel the Commanding Officer of the 1st Lancashire Fusiliers, who had been in Tianjin in 1937–8, and suddenly he was 2nd

Lieutenant Harold V. Bridge. After initial detachment as a liaison officer with the Chinese Army in North-East Burma he joined Force 136 (SOE)[36] in Burma and spent the rest of the war being dropped behind the Japanese lines to organise the Burmese tribes, before getting out to India and starting the routine again.

I had had my seventh birthday party in March 1941 in Tianjin; I was still the only son of my parents and was carefree, with minor worries as to my toys: a rather large American 'O' gauge Lionel Lines train set and an extensive collection of 'Britain's Ltd' toy soldiers.

The British Municipal Emergency Corps (BMEC) had its inaugural parade in May, when my Uncle Alwyne Ogden CMG OBE (Consul-General) took the salute from the steps of the Kailan Mining Administration on Meadows Road. My great friend Brian Calvert had his eighth birthday party on 15th June 1941. This I was invited to; I was often at Brian's as his parents and mine were great tennis players, and the Calverts had a tennis court in their garden, so Brian and I often played together, if only because our parents were in another room having a drink.[37]

I had started at the Tianjin Grammar School in January 1940 and had fallen into a routine: a rickshaw picked me up in the morning from the Court Hotel on Victoria Road and I was taken to school. The rickshaw 'boy' returned at tea-time to take me home. The grammar school had English-born teachers, Mr Woodall being the Headmaster, and used a British curriculum and the normal three terms. The Easter holidays usually spanned a fortnight, and were mostly spent in Beijing, staying at the Hotel des Wagon Lits and meandering round the 'Forbidden City'. Summer holidays were in Beidaihe, staying in the 'Bridge' compound and walking round the beach, messing around in boats and with an occasional sortie on a donkey to the Western Hills, a ridge running to the west of the village of Beidaihe.

In July and August 1941 I was at our property in Beidaihe as planned. My mother was expecting a baby in October, and spent most of her time on the beach or sitting on the veranda of the big house playing mah-jong, or just talking or having tea with her friends. I anticipated the forthcoming birth with some misgiving, because it was pretty obvious that I would have to share amah, and for all my life she had been at my beck and call. I viewed with some scepticism the fact that her priority from now would be the new arrival.

Anyhow, three of my cousins, Ken, Arthur and Douglas (their father was Harold), were older than I, roughly by two, four and six years respectively, but they, too, were spending their time at Beidaihe with their mother Hilda. They were set to head off to Canada and school while their father was at war. We had a hut down one of the gullies and a great time was being had by all. Riding the long-suffering donkeys, kept by one of the gardeners in the stable block, swimming in the sea, rowing or sailing the boats, fishing, playing tennis and generally mucking about filled our days. We were sleeping rough in the hut most nights until we realised that the small bungalow had no guests in it and Douglas broke in, so we transferred our sleeping arrangements to the beds in the bungalow. Much more comfortable. Despite being surrounded by uncles, aunts and parents, life was blissful and carefree. There was talk of war by the adults, but to us boys it could be happening on another planet.

Suddenly it was late August and Mum thought she would be better near a hospital. So suddenly the summer holiday was over. The train journey back from Beidaihe involved about half an hour's journey to the junction with the main line and a change of trains to get the express to Tianjin

East Station. We sat in first-class carriages but there was no catering on the train, only the well-stocked hampers we had brought with us, and when we stopped at Tangshan there were hawkers on the platform offering a variety of food, from steaming dumplings to fried batter sticks to cooked whole chickens. I had my eyes on the toffee apples.

'Can I have some money to buy sticky apples?' I asked hopefully as the train puffed to a stop into Tongshan Station. 'I've not had one for ages.'

'All right' Mum said with a smile, 'But take Funainai with you, you will find her on the train in the first third-class carriage, and she can buy some "red" chicken as well from that other man over there.' She handed me some money, and as we sat in the carriage I heard my father tease her.

'I thought you never let Ronald eat anything from a stall, Margot. What has come over you?'

Mum laughed. 'Oh, it's quite safe. The apples are dipped in boiling sugar and the chickens are cooked in boiling fat and soya sauce. That kills all the germs. Also the money is being touched by Funainai.'

I did not know really what she meant by germs and did not care. I was soon stuffing an apple on the end of a stick into my mouth whilst Funainai bargained for the chicken. Suddenly the engine whistled and we rushed to get back on board the train before it left the station.

Then, as the railway line ran across the countryside, there were three-storey pill boxes every mile or so, manned by whichever military was in power to protect the railway from bandits, as it ran through orchards of apples and pears. I gazed out of the window eating chicken, a sugared apple and being chided by Funainai for getting sticky sugar on my clothes. We spoke together in Chinese, which we had always used because Funainai could not speak English, and in fact the nearest she could get to my name was Lonard. She seemed very old to me. She was plump, dark-haired and always wore dark blue trousers and blue smocks daily. These became more and more padded each day as the winter set in. She wore black felt slippers on her tiny feet – the result of the custom of foot-binding, which the Manchu had tried to ban in the 17th century, and even Empress Cixi had issued an edict against it (1902). But habit and custom die hard in China. Funainai, however, tottered when she walked, and I was always able to get away from her. I could always get what I wanted from her too. In her eyes I was the eldest son and could therefore do no wrong. I had probably traded on this fact with all the staff, who had worked for my parents for as long as I could remember. Having said that, Dad at an early age told me to always look after the staff because you never knew when they could help you. A concept I have held to all my life, and it has never let me down.

The train drew into the Tianjin East Station, located in the Italian Concession. We piled out into three rickshaws, while the baggage was in the capable hands of porters. It was about a two-mile ride from the station to our flat on the first floor at the Bund side of the Court Hotel. The Court Hotel had been founded by Captain P. Laen in 1860, and boasted a fives court, a billiard room and seven bedrooms. A second floor had been added after the Boxer Rebellion, and a new three-storey wing, allowing the room count to go up to sixty. The hotel had originally opened on to the Bund, later changed in 1922 to make the entrance open off Victoria Road. The hotel was owned by Hotung Land Ltd, one of the companies of which my father was a director. The Hotel Manager's contract was 'home' on leave to Europe every five years, and he had elected in 1938 to go back to France. With no temporary manager in sight my father and mother, with one child – me – had had to fill the gap and moved into the manager's flat from our own flat in Race Course Road. When the European War started in 1939 the manager wrote to say he would not be returning, and thus by default we still lived in the hotel flat, with Dad keeping a distant supervisory role over the hotel staff.

Life in the British Concession settled into its normal routine, although I was saddened to find on return from Beidaihe that 'Spot', our wire-haired terrier, had just passed away, having caught distemper while we were on holiday. My father went back to his office down Victoria Road. My mother settled back to sit out the last few weeks before the baby came and I went off to school. I found the Grammar School far more exciting than Miss Stuart's, and the departure for school was always dramatic, with Funainai in tears and me feeling very grown-up leaving her behind. On Sunday we usually went to church at All Saints, followed by a short walk down Meadows Road to my maternal grand-parents. Mum was always pleased to see her parents and Granny Fleet enjoyed fussing over her daughter.

We all heard about the distant war in Europe and North Africa though letters from home were not so frequent. There was a ritual of listening to the BBC News each evening, although given the BBC's policy of constantly changing the broadcast frequencies, tuning in was a tiresome chore, and the first half of the news was often missed as we twiddled the dial.

I used the term 'home' as naturally as all adults used it, even though I had never been to England. I understood the possible Japanese threat but I gathered that the general feeling was that it would never grow to be more than an irritant, as it had been in 1939. I was very conscious that my mother had gathered some like-minded ladies, and on one day a week they met to have coffee while they tore bales of white calico into bandages for the British Army. Mum even designed a winder that would wind bandages, which I helped the carpenter to make. I wanted to help but could manage only the odd day, because I was at school. I managed to contribute a little, as I joined up in the Noble Order of British Spitfires (NOBS) which raised money to buy Spitfires for the Royal Air Force. All the ladies also knitted socks and balaclava helmets in Navy and Air Force blue, as well as khaki. They also sewed items for sale in the hotel to cover the costs involved. These gatherings were a sign of the changes that had been forced on the community. I was not fully aware of the nuances of the war and the worries of my parents. Mum had always had a weekly charity sale of quite exquisite embroidery done by blind Chinese women living and working at Yenching, an American mission school in Beijing, to raise funds for that community; this she continued but her profits now went partially to the war effort.

It was difficult to get very emotional about things that happened to other countries far beyond the sea, which I knew about only from an atlas, although I had an idea of the distances involved from the ship's timetables. I found the arrival of my little brother Roger far more dramatic. Though when I first was taken to see the new arrival I did not think much of him: chubby with a fat red face, who bawled as I squeezed his hand. He would not be able to play for some years, but I could see that he was the centre of attention for all adults. My Aunt Hilda and my three cousins Ken, Art and Doug set off to Shanghai on their journey to Victoria, Canada, although they only got as far as Shanghai before the war in the Far East started, which they spent in Chapei Camp as British internees of the Japanese.

I had joined the Wolf Cubs six months earlier and that

was really exciting, I had read the Fieldcraft Manual from cover to cover and then slowly learnt the contents. Dad was the Assistant Commissioner for Boy Scouts in North China, and I was allowed to join the Cubs just after my seventh birthday because I had learnt all the rules, from the first aid to the knots in the handbook. My first full parade was the week after we got back to Tianjin from holiday in September 1941.[38] It was all great fun, but had only been going for three months or so when everything changed dramatically and life as I knew it suddenly became a memory. Meanwhile, for the first time since the Cenotaph had been built there was no resident British Army battalion, and so Armistice Day went ahead with Guides, Scouts, Cubs and the British Municipal Emergency Corps.

4

The Second World War Comes to North China

The British decided to publish a list of priorities for eligibility for sea passages in the event of a sudden need to evacuate. This caused ill feeling amongst the British community. Some men married to Chinese started selling their 'seniority' on the list. Others said they did not want to go. Others said that they merited being on the 'Diplomatic' list. The haggling stopped on the 8th December 1941, a Monday morning when the Concession woke up to find the Japanese Army in complete control, and the Consul-General froze the list.

The front of the hotel had a Japanese machine gun pointing towards it. I rushed to my room door and looked down the corridor: there was a Japanese soldier with a rifle and he waved me to go back to my room. I went back in and sat on the bed, terrified. Had they taken Mum? Had they taken the baby? What was going to happen to me? I was left alone in my room for what seemed like hours. Nobody came near me and I was hungry and a little frightened, so I hid beneath the bed, just in case!

Then the door opened and I heard Mum's voice; she sounded as scared as I was. 'Ronald, Ronald where are you?' I got up from under the bed as she came into the room to tell me that I would not be going to school. She went on to say that she did not know what was happening, but had ordered the cook to make breakfast and serve it in their bedroom. This last seemed a very good idea to me, because I had foreseen my morning porridge going down the pan and the threat of hunger for the rest of the day lingered.

'What about Dad?' I asked as we walked along the corridor.

'He has been arrested and taken away by four Japanese soldiers, to be questioned,' she told me. 'I am sure he will be back soon.' In the event he was held for a week by the Japanese Military Police in the Masonic Hall on Race Course Road.

By this time we were in her room, where Roger was in his cot gurgling. He was two months old to the day. I kept asking questions, including the fact that I had not seen Funainai about.

'Most of the servants have been sent away,' Mum said. 'Funainai has gone to her relatives' house.'

'But she didn't say goodbye,' I wailed. Life without Funainai would be awful, as she was like another indulgent aunt. I had momentarily forgotten that I now had to share her with Baby Roger.

'She had to go at once. The Japanese soldiers sent her off with the others. They left only the cook to do breakfast,' Mum explained. 'Maybe they will let her back later.' Mum was trying to cheer me up and she succeeded. Especially when she announced that the Grammar School had closed until further notice.

Later in the day we found that my grandfather, 'Bert' Fleet, had been taken from his house in Meadows Road at breakfast and was also in the cells. Granny Fleet had been left on her own.

It was a *fait accompli*, and resistance would have been impossible. There had been no fewer than 30,000 Japanese soldiers around Tianjin, and the British Municipal Emergency Corps – all of two hundred part-time 'military' businessmen – would not have made much impression on the Imperial forces in a battle. To avoid a needless slaughter, the Corps were voluntarily disarmed, and the Rising Sun – or 'Poached Egg' – took control. All adult male Britons were rounded up and after a night in the cells in the Gordon Hall they were now incarcerated in the Masonic Hall on Race Course Road, where they would remain for up to four months.

By March 1942 most of the adult English males had been allowed home to their wives; very few of them were of military age, as those in that category had already left to join the British Army in the summer of 1941, to serve in Europe or the Middle East, although events meant that they virtually all ended up in Burma. Dad, being a businessman with no technical qualifications, and therefore not considered a potential saboteur, was released; he then tried to carry on the business by selling the goods that the company still had in its warehouses. The Chinese staff still required paying, and I detected that finance was tight. Those who remained in Japanese detention tended to be engineers by profession, and so considered capable of sabotaging facilities, and thus posing a potential threat to Nippon.

Initially, house arrest was the order of the day and we were confined to the house after dark. But by April 1942 the Japanese had decreed that we were to keep Tokyo time, which meant advancing clocks by two hours, and they had also issued obligatory red armbands with the character 'ying', which was the nearest they could get to 'English',[39] and formal curfew hours were established. Ironically, the Japanese did not understand Chinese customs or traditions; red was the colour of celebration for the Chinese, and 'ying' also meant 'victorious' or 'winner'.

Dad came home one day and told Mum about the armbands. The both laughed as they knew what the translation meant. 'Trust them to make a mistake like that, but, we can all go round proudly wearing them now.'

'I could remember Grandpa Bridge had told me that in Chinese the word *Ying* meant conquering race,' I put in. 'But, everybody says that Japan is winning.'

'They are not winning the propaganda war,' Dad replied. 'They probably didn't realise it.'

'Stop telling Ronald things like that,' Mum interrupted, 'He might repeat them unwittingly to someone else.'

Dad slapped me on the back. 'Just remember that we must still wear the armbands whenever we go out. Roger has one that can be pinned to his bib. It tells the world that we are English.' The Americans could also have a laugh. Their red armbands had the character 'Mei', which was the nearest the Japanese could get to 'America'. 'Mei' meant 'beautiful' or 'good'. The word 'country' in Chinese was 'Guo', which was nearly always added when talking.

I, as an eight-year-old, was not considered a threat by the Japanese: no minder or police escort for me. Consequently I often visited my maternal grandmother in her house on Meadows Road. Her husband was kept in the Masonic Hall Detention Centre until the end of March 1942 'under guard', although she was able to get small food parcels to him in January and February 1942. Grandpa Fleet was released after just under four months due to age and infirmity. (He had suffered a hernia after being pushed over by a Japanese soldier in December 1941.) After a couple of months, Funainai was allowed back to be Roger's amah, and to look after my clothes, but it was never the same for me. A chapter of my young life was over and I had been propelled a long way, and fast, into early adulthood.

We were allowed to visit my Uncle Alwyne Ogden, the British Consul-General, only on rare occasions. He, his wife Jessie (née Bridge, Dad's elder sister), their daughter Anne and son Brian were virtually locked up in the Consul-General's House at 1 Race Course Road.[40] The sentry on their gate ensured that they kept to their curfew hours, which were more stringent than ours. It was always nice to visit my cousins, as they had bicycles and I could ride round the garden. The Ogdens had been allowed to keep their servants because the Japanese seemed to respect diplomatic niceties.

Mum and I were able to visit my paternal Grandmother, who was seventy-five and frail. She had moved in with Freda (née Bridge, Dad's eldest sister) on Parks Road near the Union Church with her husband, my uncle by marriage Tullis Lewis. He was temporarily held in the Masonic Hall by the Japanese Army; he was an engineer and part-time Fire Brigade Chief. (He only turned out if there was a big fire.) That absence caused endless worry to his wife and mother-in-law. Mum during her visits always got dragged into that conversation, which allowed me to sneak up to Uncle Tullis's train room and play.

Dad's two RCA Victor Radios, his Ford V8 and the Rover car were confiscated, although he was given a receipt that they would be returned at the cessation of the conflict. (As an aside, I sent copies off to the Japanese Ambassador in London in the year 2000. To be told that Emperor Akihito

33

was now on the throne and the Japanese Government did not accept the validity of the signature of one of Former Emperor Hirohito's officers!) One of the radios was later returned with the short-wave capability removed, and then confiscated again in March 1943, never to be seen again.

The British Tianjin Grammar School was requisitioned, along with all the other British municipal buildings. The older grammar school pupils were all told in January 1942 that they could call at the school to collect their books. The Japanese Military Authorities had given permission, and on Saturday us children assembled in the school. The school hall was packed and Mr Woodall the Headmaster came in and sent us all to the classrooms to collect our books. As soon as a form got into its room the door was locked. The teachers helped as they spent the next couple of hours filling in forms, and waiting for the Japanese to let them go. The Headmaster then ushered us all out into the playground where the officer in charge was going to address us. A red carpet was laid out to the side entrance ready for his arrival.

However, his adjutant decided that this was not impressive enough and the red carpet was wheeled round to the main entrance.

Mr Woodall got in a quick but very loud word to the assembled children. 'Be very serious. Do not laugh,' knowing how the Japanese hated any, even imagined, ridicule at their expense.

Through the interpreter the Major began, but the interpreter seemed to be stuck on a few words which were repeated over and over. 'Very sorry we must take school from you. We do not want to take school but Military Orders say we must. Very sorry but Military Orders must be obeyed. You continue your education somewhere else. Very sorry.'

My books came home with me in the rickshaw.

My parents did not have much time to teach me anything, Dad was constantly being summoned to the Japanese
Headquarters. The trouble seemed to be that one of Dad's
companies, Hotung Land, had a contract to look after the
buildings of the former British Army Barracks. I overheard
my parents' conversation and realised the issue: the Japanese
were convinced that Dad had the keys to the safes in the barracks. I never found out whether the Japanese thought that
the safes contained arms, bullion or just money. Anyhow, by
the end of 1942 the Japanese were very frustrated and used
explosives, to find that indeed the safes lay empty.

I did get stuck into my algebra and geography books.
Mum was finding it very hard without servants to look after
a baby and a near-disobedient boy – me – under the pre-
vailing conditions. I had to obey the rules of the curfew and
stay in after dark. I was fortunate in that I had the run of the
hotel, but there was really very little to do, but still I did not
have to get up early because there was no school to go to.

After a few weeks boredom set in, and then, after a lot
of haggling with the Military Authorities, there was an
attempt made to educate the British and American children by establishing a school at a large private house in the
British Concession, occupied by Wilfred Pryor, the Acting
Chief Manager of the Kailan Mining Administration and
his family. His daughter Gillian was a little older than I, and
his youngest daughter Shirley two years my junior.

The Pryors' drawing room was transformed into a class-
room, allocated to Form Three, and seventeen of us trooped
in every morning. The floor was beautiful wood-block
parquet and impressed me. All the furniture had been moved
out, chairs and a large blackboard replacing them. My seat
was close to the French window overlooking the garden, and
I spent many hours, particularly during French or English

Literature, working out what the Pryors grew in their garden. I noted with approval that there was evidence that they used straw to cover up their grape vines, climbing roses and clematis. I could still remember Grandfather Bridge's exhortation that to grow European plants in the harsh North China climate one needed to wrap the plants with straw and lay them on the ground[41] during the winter months.

School continued each Monday to Friday from just after nine to five. Three lessons in the morning, and two plus games in the afternoon. The garden was not big enough for teams; use of the Minyuan Ground was negotiated as it was not far. But using different houses meant that teachers had to cycle or use a rickshaw between the various classes. It was considered safe or more controllable for the adult teacher to move than the children. Thus games were back on the timetable.

Fraternisation continued erratically with French friends, who had all declared themselves Petain supporters, and thus allies of Japan and hence outside Japan's regulations. Other European nationals surreptitiously tried to help. Social ties with Germans and of course the Japanese were cut completely.

Whilst I was in the hotel, the lack of guests meant that I had all the corridors to myself. Mum, concentrating on Roger and finding washing clothes by hand a real chore, could afford me little time and hence supervision had evaporated, allowing me to run riot. I took to watching the Japanese sentries on the back yard of the hotel and on the front. The latter were relatively friendly and even on occasions offered sweets. The back overlooking the Bund was quite different. They had a machine gun in a sandbag emplacement. I tried to get near to see if it was loaded on a number of occasions, but that always woke the soldier up and he shouted and waved his arms. I realised that it was a step too far, and scarpered in terror.

The Chinese and Sikh constables of the former British Municipal Police continued with their duties under Japanese officers, as did the Russian Sergeants. Some categories within the population, although technically British, were free of any restrictions and did not have to wear armbands: those British citizens not considered European enough, women married to Japanese or their allies, Chinese wives of Maritime Customs officers, and their children under five. Maritime Customs officers themselves were treated like the rest of us. In July 1942 diplomatic and selected people were notified they would be exchanged, but would have to travel to Shanghai first.

The British diplomats, who included Uncle Alwyne and family as well as others, were augmented on the 'exchange' by adults who could wangle their way onto the passenger list. They were all taken to Shanghai in early August and on 16th August 1942 they sailed from Shanghai on the *Kamakura Maru*, known by then as the *Wangle Maru*, to Lourenço Marques.[42] This was in Mozambique, a Portuguese colony, hence neutral, where the actual exchange for a similar number of Japanese citizens took place on the Swedish SS *Gripsholm*.

In early September I learnt that the Pryors' house had been requisitioned, so now school was 'off' for all those under ten. Grandpa Fleet was back with his wife in their Meadows Road house, where they stayed for the next six months or so. I used to go virtually daily in roughly school hours to be taught by Grandpa Fleet, mainly mathematics, history and geography. As no names for streets in Tianjin were allowed by the Japanese, his house, which had been 143 Meadows Road, was now House 143 Road Number 20.

It was three-quarters of a mile from where we lived in the Court Hotel and I only had three roads to cross to get there; cars were few and most goods were carried in human-pulled carts. Mum was tied up with the baby and, because of the performance of getting him into a pram, I said to Mum that I could walk to Grandpa's on my own. I enjoyed the freedom to be by myself. My grandparents' house was spacious, with Grandpa's study at ground level off the garden; he had a weakness for growing flowers, especially poinsettias and hollyhocks. I used to think it strange – the short and the tall – but they were rarely out together. The floor above had the bedrooms, and I used to use the small room above the entrance if I stayed a night.

Dad had done business with a certain Russian-Swiss Company, Bryners, that specialised in shipping and forwarding. He was apprehensive as to how things were going to work out so decided safeguards were necessary, and as a precaution contacted them. Mr Bryner[43] allowed the Bridge family silver, linen and upright piano (which had been buried during the Boxer trouble in 1900) and valuable furniture to be stored in wooden packing cases under at least 40 tons of coal, and there it stayed for the duration of hostilities, in the Bryner warehouses or godowns. The amount of coal went up and down but the boxes were never exposed. Mum was dismayed when it was collected in 1945, as the linen was black, but she recovered it and it washed up well. Some is still in use as I write seventy-odd years later.

The apprehension about possessions rubbed off on me, for whilst I knew that my toy soldiers were portable, the same could not be said of my train sets. I had been told some days before that Aunt Freda and her husband were staying in Tianjin, and not going to camp, because old Granny Bridge was excused internment and they were being allowed to stay behind as her custodians.

When going in and out of my parents' bedroom I noticed Dad's Browning 0.32 on top of the wardrobe. I think he had forgotten where it was; I realised that it might be, to the Japanese, 'big trouble', so I smuggled it into the train room while packing up the train, wrapped it in an oily cloth and stuffed it behind loose bricks and carefully screwed the train table back. I was only just in time at packing up the train and deliberately forgot anything about the revolver.

The Japanese Army then deemed it necessary to implement a new policy: the concentration of Allied civilians from isolated premises into one place, especially if they were living in places where they might 'spy' on troop or ship movements. People who owned their own property were sometimes able to stay in it. But our flat at the back of the Court Hotel overlooked the Bund, and was considered a strategic location by the Japanese Military. They feared that we might count ship and troop movements. So we were given a few days' notice before being forcibly relocated.

Whilst the armband curfew regulations remained in force, the venue chosen for the Bridge family, and those Britons whose houses the Japanese Army had requisitioned, was the Talati House Hotel, owned and run by a British-Indian family, the Dhunjishahs. This was effectively requisitioned and filled with Allied citizens in September 1942, although the enforced 'guests' were invited by Japan to pay for their own food and accommodation. I, my parents and brother exchanged the luxury of our 'company' flat for the cramped quarters of two small single hotel rooms. Sadly, Funainai had to be paid off as a result of the move to Talati House. We had become accustomed to the almost daily changes and upheavals. The new rooms were much the same distance from Granny and Grandpa's house, in which they were allowed to stay. So, my erratic teaching by a 65-year-old pensioner could continue.

Christmas 1942 came somewhat muted: few presents could be exchanged, church services allowed only by daylight. Mum was always strained and almost short-tempered. I managed to get out of her much of the reason why. When the Japanese had taken over on 8th December 1941 she had been carrying my brother, then two months old. She was being ushered rather fast along a corridor and stairs with the usual 'Speedo' cry when she tripped and fell. The shouts reached a crescendo and the soldier, thinking she had deliberately tried to delay matters, hit her with the butt of his rifle, right across her kidneys. I think Roger had sensed that something was wrong and tended to cry more, possibly thinking that he could summon help. Mum had then got to my room, but felt that there was no need for me to know.

When rumours first began circulating within the city that the American and British civilians would soon be shipped out, nobody really believed it. I just hoped that we would be able to move to my grandparents' house; that was not on the agenda though. My ninth birthday came and went completely uncelebrated, and then on March 12th 1943 each adult Briton received a letter from O. Joerg, Consul for Switzerland,[44] in charge of British, American and Dutch interests, enclosing a copy of the letter that he had received from the Japanese Consul-General.[45] Internship in a Japanese camp was now the order of the day.

Readers will note that the Japanese and Swiss Consular authorities, in communicating with each other, did not use the then language of diplomacy, French, but rather a style of written English familiar to Whitehall's Civil Service and the British Military Staff Colleges; indeed, the precepts of

Victoria's British educationalists had percolated to every
strata of almost every nation's endeavour in the Far East.
Britain had been around for a long time and had intended
to run things the British way. The 'loss of face' with the
fall of Hong Kong and then of Singapore had made a huge
dent in Britain's standing in the Far East, and knowing the
thought processes of Eastern cultures it would probably
never recover.

The instructions attached to the Swiss letter allowed
each prospective internee to ship a case, a single bed and
a few books, plus one sewing machine per 100 prospective inmates. These to be ready for an inspection by the
Kempetai one week before the individual's departure, when
the Japanese Army conducted a very thorough and ran-
sacking search, which ensured that the cases were no longer
able to be secured properly and so the contents were largely
pilfered on the later journey. All other possessions were to
be locked away and the Kempetai would place seals on the
locks, where things would be left untouched until the war
finished, no sooner uttered than realised to be a hollow
promise. Houses and flats were to have a detailed inventory
made of all contents and the keys lodged with the Japanese
Army for safekeeping. There was no need to include cars or
radios as separate receipts had already been given when they
were confiscated.

Imperial Japanese Consulate

11ᵗʰ March 1943

Dear Colleague,
I have the honour to inform you that owing to military
requirements enemy nationals residing in Tientsin who are
American, British, Dutch and Belgian citizens are ordered

41

to leave for Weihsien,[46] Shandong Province to reside in an assembly.

The party is scheduled to proceed to Weihsien[47] in three groups, the first leaving on the 23rd, the second group on the 28th and the third group on the 30th instant. (March 1943.)

I should be much obliged if you will kindly inform those enemy nationals under your charge to this effect. Instructing them that they should prepare for the assembly in conformity with the instructions attached herewith.

I have the honour to be,\
Sir and dear colleague,\
Your obedient servant\
Tomotsune Ohta

My Grandparents, Bert and Elizabeth Fleet, told us that they were scheduled for the 23rd March departure. Whilst Mum, Dad, Roger and I were on the 30th March; my paternal grandmother, Minnie Bridge, could stay behind[48] with her eldest daughter Freda and Freda's husband, Tullis, both of whom, as I had already found out, were excused camp to look after her in their house. There was then frantic activity to catalogue inventories of house contents (although in our case that had been done when we were turfed out of our flat in the Court Hotel), buy suitcases, pack trunks and crate beds. This 'deep sea' baggage was to arrive at Weihsien in early April. Those that had not been relocated were told to inventory their houses and leave the lists and the keys with the Kempetai.

5

Destination Weihsien

On 30th March 1943 we had breakfast and then assembled our suitcases. It was still quite cool in the mornings and evenings at the end of March. Mum told me to put on shorts, long socks, lace-up shoes, shirt, sweater and coat. I felt hot walking to the assembly point but I was told to keep them on as they were more to carry and I could lose them otherwise. Mum had bought stacks of tinned food, and I could not really see the reason for that, but she was insistent that it go with us. In all this bustle, my Britains Ltd toy soldiers had not been found a home. I was determined not to leave them behind so I stuffed my pockets with as many as I could; the coat I had been complaining about proved very useful in this respect, with four more pockets.

We then piled into four rickshaws, Dad, me with a suitcase, Mum and Roger, and another with dismantled pram and more suitcases. The rickshaws and their 'boys' had been hired until the train was scheduled to depart. Our first stop was the former British Army barracks, which Mum thought idiotic, as it was on the west of the Concession, and further than the East Station. We duly arrived at the barracks, where it was everybody out to form lines in the parade ground; the Japanese Army had taken over, and was going to conduct yet another search of the contents of all suitcases. It was obvious it was not going to be an administrative-only stop. The rickshaw boys were sent off, but not before all of Mum's tins were put in the reassembled Pedigree pram and the mattress replaced. Mum had over-estimated the capacity of the pram in buying her tins, which was now full, and then Roger was placed precariously on the top. He now had no rail to stop him rolling out. Dad remarked 'Margot, you will not be able to tear round corners or our youngest son will be on the road.'

Dad, who had moved around a bit, came and reported that there were about 300 people waiting. After a couple of hours we told that we would be walking to the station. Rickshaws were now banned. So with the rickshaw boys paid off, we set out of the barrack gates almost as the sun was setting. We were greeted by a huge Chinese 'Rent-a-Crowd' who hurled rubbish, abuse and spat at us. I heard words I had picked up from Chinese boys and which were banned in polite company, not that I had ever used them. I also knew that the Japanese propaganda machine had been dispensing a large number of bank notes in their own currency.

Dad was carrying Mum's suitcase as well as his own. I had my small pigskin Revelation expanding case, which was indeed 'expanded', and a bag with the overflow of groceries. The road used ran mainly east through the French Concession then north along Rue de France to the International Bridge to cross the Hai Ho River and then along past the main Post Office to the railway station.

The attitude of the crowd had changed as we turned on to Rue de France, suddenly turning sullen and very quiet, and you could see some, mainly women, crying. It was obvious that the Japanese had run out of money. Those that they had paid did their 'Rent-a-Crowd' bit, while those that had not had their palms greased reverted to the normal behaviour of a North Chinese crowd: inquiring, querulous, apprehensive of the change they were seeing in their midst, and with an inherent appreciation that things were never going to be the same again.

The walk seemed to go on forever, but I was wrestling with a suitcase and a bag, Dad had two and Mum was just pushing the pram and keeping Roger on it with difficulty. The walk seemed to take at least two hours, but I subsequently discovered from a map that it was only just over two miles.

When we arrived at the East Station there was more waiting, but we were allowed to purchase food from the station stalls. Then we were loaded on to a train, not in the 1st-class carriages, nor in the 2nd with their padded seats and wooden backs, but into 3rd which had wooden seats with wooden back rests. I had only been in such a carriage before when I had surreptitiously visited Funainai on journeys to Beijing or Beidaihe. The English *always* travelled 1st class, or so I thought until that moment.

The train set off with much whistling and trundled through the night, arriving at dawn at Tsinan, a railway junction in Shandong where we had to change trains. I and others tried to stretch our legs after the cramped conditions in the 3rd-class carriage overnight. But on approaching the boundaries of the station forecourt a guard burst into life. There was no need to understand Japanese: the wavering rifle and bayonet said it all. We had to stay close to the station. The Japanese Ariska rifle with bayonet fitted was over 5 foot long and almost seemed to dwarf the soldier carrying it.

Then inevitable chaos occurred when we were ushered onto the 3rd-class benches again. The train was older and marked 'Qingdao'.[49] After nearly five hours we stopped at a station; the sign on the platform read 'Weihsien'.

The Japanese guards shouted 'evelybody get off', and then immediately added 'Speedo, Speedo!' So we got the message, and then in the station forecourt everybody lined up to be counted, clutching their suitcases. There were a number of recounts before the guards agreed that there was no one missing. Then we had to climb into about ten Japanese Army trucks.

It was very uncomfortable squatting on my suitcase in the truck. I was squashed between my mother on one side and my father on the other and little Roger was whining away as he sat on Mum's knee. Around us the truck was full of people who had come down in the train with us from Tianjin, and no one could sit down properly. There were about thirty people of all ages, some of the men standing and trying to keep their balance as the vehicle swayed when the driver swerved to avoid the potholes and hopefully not break an axle. The road deteriorated rapidly as houses gave way to open country, fields that would be filled with stalks carrying cobs of Indian maize and kaoliang come the autumn, although in the spring all that stood out was the burial mounds of hundreds of Chinese graves. These I had seen all over my journeys in China. The tradition at that time being that each year more earth was piled on the burial mound. The amount of land for crops diminished, while the population grew.

I tugged my father's sleeve and asked, 'Dad when will we get there?'

'Soon' he replied quickly, patting me on the shoulder.

'But, when we will get something to eat, Dad?'

'I am not sure. But, I would hope that it will not be too long,' Dad added.

'Oh, good,' I said. 'Roger will be happy too when he has had some food, although he seems content enough sucking his blanket.'

We had been bumping along an ever-worsening road for, it seemed to me, ages, but had probably only been half an hour or so, and I wanted to get down to stretch my legs. Behind us stretched out a long line of a dozen trucks carrying the rest of the passengers from our train. I had normally only travelled on a road by rickshaw or in a car, usually my father's Rover, and it had been a lot more comfortable than sitting on a suitcase in the back of an open truck.

Next to the driver of the truck behind I saw that, instead of a seat, there was a large metal contraption, smoking madly. I turned to my father, rudely interrupting him while he was talking to another man, and asked 'What is that thing next to the driver? Why is there not another seat like you had in your car?'

Sighing, my father explained patiently. 'That is a boiler beside the driver which burns charcoal to make carbon monoxide gas for the engine as the Japanese are very short of petrol. If you look at our truck, as well as all the others, they have the same charcoal boilers. The poor road surface, the substitute fuel and the overloaded trucks are all conspiring to lengthen the time it will take to get to Weihsien.'

'We are surely nearly there,' my mother interjected, to prevent my quest for knowledge getting any more irritating to adults.

We were travelling along the valley of a small river when quite suddenly a 16-foot wall, topped with barbed wire and broken glass, with a pillbox on the corner, appeared on the right. Some 150 yards along the wall it was pierced by a gateway, and in contrast to the fields around us there were trees behind the wall. The massive wooden gates had three large Chinese characters above, which one of the men rapidly translated out loud: 'Courtyard of the Happy Way'. Although I spoke Chinese adequately I had not mastered many characters, so I could not read the caption. Funainai was illiterate, and I had been left with spoken Chinese. The plan was the written word would come later.

'Will it be a Happy Way?' chorused Dad and some of the passengers, while we were driven through the gate and up an incline to stop in front of a bungalow block. Ours was the second of ten or so trucks that had brought the three hundred people from the Tianjin train.

When all the vehicles had stopped, some Japanese guards emerged from a low building and told us all to disembark, mainly by signs but using what I suspected was the only near-English word they knew: 'Speedo'. The best part of an hour was taken up with milling around finding lost children or baggage. Still no sign of food and I was really getting very hungry.

In addition to the guards, there were a number of fellow inmates loitering around. These were the men and women who had arrived in Weihsien a week or ten days before. A group, mainly bachelors or those whose wives had not been interned because they had got away on a ship or were foreign nationals, had formed themselves, in true British fashion, into a Committee to run the camp, with the encouragement of the Commandant. Dad recognised two business friends from Tianjin, Ted McClaren of Butterfield & Swire, who was the Tianjin Manager of one of the British shipping companies who controlled the China coast trade, the other Tom Waters, manager of the Asiatic Petroleum Company (the local Shell Oil Company subsidiary). Dad shipped goods in the former's ships and used to play rugger with Ted; he also leased land to APC for their bulk oil installation.

Tom spoke to my father and said, 'Leo, I see that you have all your family here. Any trouble over accommodation and I will see what I can do. Ted here runs the Discipline side of the Camp Committee, whilst I have drawn the "Accommodation brief".'

Meanwhile the new arrivals had been herded across in front of the Church to the softball field, an empty space about three-quarters the size of a football pitch. Having had, wearily, to pick up our cases again on orders from the guards, we then went on to the field where we were lined up because the Camp Commandant wished to address us. Then a short bandy-legged man, in the uniform of the Japanese Consular police (whose black uniforms contrasted with the Imperial Japanese Army's greenish khaki), stood up. He was full of self-importance, and the crowd was instructed to pay careful attention.

'I am Captain Tsukiyama, and I am commandant of this Civilian Assembly Centre, Weihsien. You do as I say and no trouble. Big big trouble if you do not obey. Speak only English or Japanese, no Chinese otherwise big trouble. You all arrive here today. You will be well looked after. You will be given block and room numbers now and people who arrive before you will show you the way.'

Captain Tsukiyama had chosen to address us in Japanese, although he had been Japan's Vice-Consul in Honolulu for the previous three years, and each sentence had to be translated by the interpreter, who spoke less English than the Consul himself. 'Listen now for names, from my second in command Lt Voshida.' Tsukiyama finished speaking and strode away, with his long cavalry sword occasionally hitting the ground.

Voshida began reading the litany of names, and given the interpreter's inability to separate the pronunciation of L from R, it was a tedious process. Another hour and a half and my empty stomach was rumbling loudly, as well as my boredom, which had reached its peak.

My mother's contribution was 'Be quiet! Can't you see that your brother Roger has cried himself to sleep while we wait?'

Although I had lost interest in the proceedings, I noticed the European men standing on one side, obviously earlier arrived inmates. They looked untidy and almost dirty, but it soon became clear what they were waiting for; I realised that they were the guides and as families got their accommodation and picked up their bags they were led off the field to disappear in the direction of the buildings.

Meanwhile I sat down on my brown pigskin case and looked around. I could see a watchtower on the wall, and the setting sun opposite lit up the interior, showing a machine gun poking out of the slot with a guard behind, pointing at the crowd. There was another tower further along the wall and it too had a gun also pointing at us. I was suddenly frightened and realised that the war had been brought to me. But the fear soon passed off, as I said to myself you need to win this one.

The crowd slowly thinned. Former residents of Tianjin had initially been allocated rooms in Blocks 15 to 22; our shipment's fate was now to fill these blocks, with the remainder being allocated to Blocks 35 to 42. Each block contained either six, twelve or thirteen rooms, each room 12ft (3½m) by 8ft (2⅓m) constructed of bricks laid hollow, with a tiled roof insulated by kaoliang stalks. (These resembled sugar cane but were only ½ inch thick.) Some rooms had a brick-built stove. The rooms, huts to my mind, were supposed to be capable of housing three people, and families of two adults and two to four children were supposed to get two rooms.

I stood up again as it was now getting dark and huddled closer to my father. 'When will it be our turn to go?' I whispered.

He put his arm round me and said, 'Soon we will be given our rooms.'

Then the interpreter called out 'Ruwis' – no one moved. The Japanese called out the name 'Ruwis' a couple more times, then just shrugged and marked his list.

My mother said, as my parents looked at each other, 'Surely they do not mean Freda and Tullis – their surnames are Lewis.'

'I suppose that they could have made a mistake,' my father retorted.

When the sun went down it became dark quite quickly, but also cold as it always was in March in North China. I shivered and wished our names were called out.

I tried again: 'When will it be our turn, I'm hungry. We haven't had anything since that mouldy bread at breakfast.'

Told to shut up again, I sensed my parents' unhappiness; everything was suddenly so strange. I envied my brother, who had fallen asleep in my father's arms. He was a baby, what could he understand of all this at eighteen months? I did not understand all that much of the politics of it, but I was nine years old, a cut above the three- to six-year-olds who had been causing so much trouble by getting themselves lost. We had been told that it was one room for two people, which seemed reasonable, but it would mean that I would have to share with Roger, when I had been used to a single room back in Tianjin.

Suddenly there was just my parents, Roger and me left.

Dad went off to see Voshida as he was packing up. Whilst I got on to my hobby horse 'Mum when are we going? It's cold, and I am hungry.'

'Soon' she replied.

I saw my father hesitate, and promptly thought, 'Now what else has gone wrong?' Were we going to stay on the sports field for the night? Then, I saw that Dad was talking to Voshida.

'You there what is your name? You not on list?' Voshida asked.

'Bridge' my father replied. 'Four of us me, Leo, my wife Margot and two sons Ronald and Roger.'

'Not on Rist. No Looms Reft,' Voshida snapped. He was clearly irritated and did not know what to do.

'We had orders to come to Weihsien. I have the papers here,' my father murmured, fumbling in his pocket. He passed my brother over to Mum.

He showed Voshida the papers; he grumbled but accepted the official documents. 'Only one room left for Ruwis but no show up. Bad people, no show, we find them, big trouble.'

'Freda Lewis is my sister. Her husband Tullis is with her and they are permitted to stay in their house in Tianjin to look after my mother, Mrs Minnie Bridge, who is sick and seventy-five years old,' my father explained quietly.

Voshida looked at Dad and back at his list. 'You should stay with mother,' he muttered.

'No' my father insisted proudly, 'I am not accepting special treatment. We are here and we need rooms.' I reached for his hand, not sure what was happening.

'You have Ruwis room for now.'

Tom Waters, who had been out of earshot, came across and took over where Voshida had left off, saying 'Margot and Leo, you are apparently not supposed to be here, as you are not on the Japanese list of the train passengers. I see an annotation on yet another list that you were remaining in Tianjin because your mother Mrs Minnie Bridge is listed as infirm and excused internment.'

My father then said that was indeed the case, and that he had applied, but this was the first he had heard that it had actually been agreed; of course, in fact his sister (my Aunt Freda) and her husband Tullis Lewis were the ones who stayed behind in their own house, hosting Granny Bridge to enable Freda to look after her; my father thought that their names were the ones to have been called out.

'Leo, I am afraid that you and your family will have to have the last empty room, Block 42 Room 6. It will not be too bad as one of your boys is a baby. When the dust settles we should be able to re-house you.'

I only half-caught this conversation, as my mind was on the guard towers, the guns, the barbed wire and the lack of food: I was not sure in which order.

Tom took some of what Mum was carrying and left her with the pram and Roger, then led the way. We walked through what seemed like endless little courtyards, each made up of half a dozen or more rooms with arched brick doorways. After the first few blocks Tom said 'The Tianjin kitchen is through there, Committee have kept it open with volunteers until nine. Leo you should be able to get some soup and bread to keep the wolves at bay!'

At this remark, my ears pricked up: there seemed to be a chance to fill my stomach, but I wasn't going to hold out much hope until I had at least a crust in my hands. It was a long way, or so it seemed to me as I was so tired now. Some of the blocks we had passed were larger than the others; then we came past the shower block and came to eight blocks, in pairs, each of six rooms. Last on the left was Block 42 and our room, No. 6, stood at the end.

It was a small brick room, about 12ft by 8ft, in a row of six similar rooms, with a door and window at the front. We went in and saw that there was also a small window high on the back wall. We could see other families trying to sort themselves out in adjacent blocks.

It was now nearly dark, and felt cold inside our room, which was lit only by a 25-watt light bulb, and when the luggage had been put down there was no space to move. Our trunks were not due to arrive for a week, and there were rumours that the chances of them arriving intact were slim. To no one in particular, Mum said wearily 'What are we going to sleep on?'

'For tonight, the floor,' Dad said, trying to sound cheerful. 'We can use our spare clothes as blankets and pillows. With four of us in here it should be quite cosy.'

'Do I have to undress?' I asked. 'I don't want to get cold by taking my coat off.'

'As an exception,' Mum put in, 'You can keep your clothes on tonight.' I could tell from the sound of her voice she was near to tears herself. I sniffed in sympathy. It was all so strange.

Dad got us organised and went off to find No. 1 (Tianjin) Kitchen. He returned with some bread and soup which tasted very good, despite being thin. I was so tired by then I just curled up on the earth floor, which seemed a good idea, and was rather fun, like camping with the Wolf Cubs back in Tianjin the previous summer.

'This is like a holiday. We have not had a holiday since we last stayed in our house in Beidaihe, and that was four months before this war started. Is this going to be like staying at Beidaihe?' I murmured sleepily. My head was warm on my spare sweater and I was rolled in a ball.

'I wish it was, I envy little Roger. He is curled up in his pram having had a meal and is sound asleep,' my mother whispered softly as she lay down beside me.

I was asleep in minutes and began to dream of my last holiday by the sea, when I was allowed to build a tent out of a sheet. It already seemed a lifetime away.

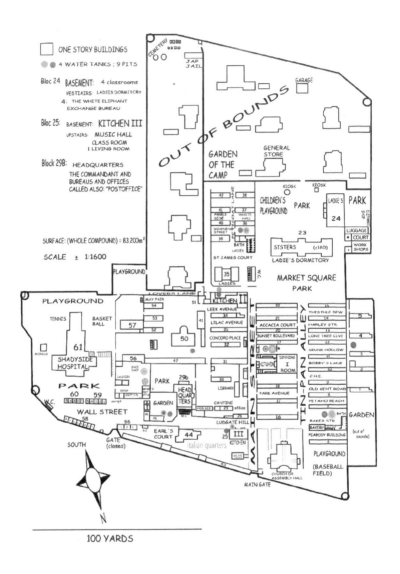

Plan of Weihsien

6

Settling in to Strange Surroundings

In spite of the rock-hard floor I slept well that first night in camp. On reflection it was not surprising, as there had been two days of travelling, a night when I had not seen a bed followed by a day without food. I woke up to hear someone knocking at the door.

'Who is that?' Mum called out nervously. 'Wait a moment. I'm coming.'

She got to her feet, and her movement woke Roger who had been lying on bundled-up clothes between Mum and Dad since daylight. Then he promptly started wailing.

'It is only me Margot' called out the familiar voice of my grandmother. 'I have just come down to see how you are and how you managed on the journey.'

It was wonderful to see her small figure outside, well wrapped in her everyday grey woollen coat. Granny was not much taller than I, just under 5 foot; she was rather rounder, but at that moment she was a comfortingly familiar figure. Her face was serene as usual and her grey hair had been drawn into a neat bun at the nape of her neck. She was wearing her usual pince-nez glasses. Mum did not look much like her, being much slimmer and 6 inches taller. Granny kissed her daughter, gave me a hug and picked up Roger who immediately stopped bawling.

'Where is Leo?' Granny asked. 'Has he gone off to get your breakfast? I was going to take you down to the kitchen. We have to use Kitchen No. 1 as we are over in Block 13 but you are in Block 42 and will have to use Kitchen No. 2. Both kitchens have dining rooms attached.'

'Last night Leo brought us our supper here, and I think he will do the same today.' Mum added quickly, 'I don't really want to take Roger to a public dining room. We haven't got a high chair for him and he will just be a nuisance if he cries all the time.'

I had only just realised the significance of Dad not being in the little hut. But if he was off getting food that was all right. I was starving hungry again and I slipped outside to watch for his coming back.

The night before, I had not really taken things in regarding my surroundings. It had been at least half dark, and I was too tired and upset to care where we were, so long as I could get food and somewhere warm to sleep. Now, as I stood outside, I realised we were in a little courtyard, with six rooms in our block and six more in the next. The path separating the two blocks was in the middle and led to the rest of the camp.

Granny pointed out that the wall on the left and in front of us divided us from where the Japanese guards lived, in the old missionary houses, and that that area was prohibited to all internees. She went on to say that the huts that we were living in had been the student quarters when Weihsien was an American Presbyterian Mission School. Founded in 1883, Weihsien played a leading role in establishing primary and secondary schools for girls throughout its mission field. The missionaries had begun with a conservative agenda of creating good Christian households at the time, and Weihsien, as it now was, had originally been just a single building; it grew to encompass a compound containing a high school, a large three-storey hospital, called Shadyside,[50] the Arts College of the Shandong Christian University, a Bible School, and residences for the missionaries and teachers. The 1911 Revolution[51] had boosted its status, followed by subsequent injections of American money. In addition to its institutions, the mission established schools and dispensaries throughout its catchment area, covering some 400 square miles around the station in Weihsien. These schools not only trained female students to become professional teachers and nurses, but also enlightened them in the local cultural sphere. Sadly, the invasion of the Japanese in 1937–8 meant that all the laboratories and operating theatres had been looted; indeed, the hospital had had all its plumbing ripped out.

Along the path I could see another three sets of buildings like ours, and then more structures beyond. More important I could see Dad walking towards us, bringing breakfast in a Chinese-type food carrier,[52] which Mum had thoughtfully packed in case there was going to be communal catering. We had only bread, weak tea and a little milk for Roger, but it tasted very good and after this I was ready to check out the neighbourhood. Mum wanted to unpack and sort out our small home, which I considered pointless until our beds arrived.

I said that I would like to go out and explore. It was obvious though that Mum was worried that I would get lost.

'Come with me,' Granny said, solving the problem. 'I can show him around and take him to our hut where Bert is and leave you in peace. Come on Ronald.'

Happy to have something to do, I followed the bustling

figure of my grandmother along the path between the blocks of rooms. We came out near Kitchen No. 2, where our meals would be prepared. The building on the left, she said, was the ladies' shower block. We walked past the kitchen and across the top of Main Street, which ran south towards the main entrance. I must have walked near or on this road last night, and said so, but Granny thought that we would have taken a route along some of the blocks to the left. Main Street was lined with mature trees, some nearly 60 feet tall. We walked only a little way before turning left past Kitchen No. 1 and then a large dining area. Each side of us were blocks of accommodation rooms, but these blocks seemed to contain about a dozen rooms. At the ends of the blocks were linking walls, so the effect was a series of courtyards. Then we came to a raised road of random granite blocks. I asked Granny why. And she said that it would keep our feet dry when the summer rains came. Granny turned south along 'Rocky Road'; I knew the direction from the position of the sun in the sky. Shortly after, we came upon a large space with no buildings but filled with different sorts of trees. Then, in front of us, was a large grey building with a bell tower in the middle tiled with the red tiles so common all over China.

'That building and the one behind it were classrooms,' Granny said.

'Does that mean I am going to school?' I asked.

Granny laughed and said 'No, the rooms are now used as dormitories for Roman Catholic priests and nuns who arrived in Weihsien at the beginning of March.'

We walked round the end of the building to another open space, but this was filled with blackened and broken desks, and laboratory equipment. There were one or two internees picking over the burnt remains in case they could find something that might be useful.

'Look, they have had a big fire, Granny,' I said.

'Yes they have, but it was done by the Japanese Army about five years ago when the Japanese were fighting the Chinese, and they destroyed the school. Such a waste.' She continued, 'The American missionaries fled and the Chinese students were either killed or sent back to their towns and villages.'

'Why did they kill the students?' I asked.

'They were innocent enough and harmless and would not have hurt anyone. But they were Chinese and there was a war on. Just like Japan has now declared war on us English.'

The block in front of us was also classrooms, but that too was now used as dormitories for priests and nuns.

'Where do you live Granny?' I asked.

'Not very far away in Block 13,' she replied. 'I am going to take you there as Grandpa should be back now from Kitchen No. 1. In the meantime I thought I would show you this area.'

'Why has he been at the kitchen? Surely, he doesn't work there?' I commented.

'Oh, yes he does. All the internees here at Weihsien have to do something for the Community, we have no servants like we all used to have before the Japanese came. I believe that the present rules excuse ladies with children under two and the one or two ladies expecting babies. I peel vegetables in No. 1 Kitchen.' We carried on walking across the near open place with all the trees.

'Granny, why are there so many different types of tree in Weihsien?'

'Because, when it was a school and college they used to teach botany, and rather than show the students pictures of trees they let them see real trees. So many of the students came from Shandong Province where there are only small trees that could almost pass for bushes,' Granny replied.

'There is a big river north of us now which is called the Yellow River or Hwang Ho. From the time of Jesus until 1853 it flowed into the Yellow Sea a couple of hundred miles south of here. Then there was a big flood which killed off the trees in Shandong Province. When the water had all flowed out to sea the river had changed its course from a place called Kaifeng and flowed north-east to the sea which meant that the Shandong hills, where Weihsien is, became south of the river.'

'There is Grandpa going in to your room,' I said as we entered the courtyard, defined by a wall between the ends of Blocks 13 and 14. When we got to the room Grandpa was surveying the pile of blankets and clothes on the floor and the packing cases alongside one wall, which had arrived the day before. He was scratching his head and studying the mess in the small space, particularly the two dismantled beds in a crate. He looked up in pleasure when we appeared in the doorway.

After hugging me and asking after Mum, Dad and Roger, he took charge.

'I will show Ronald the camp,' he said firmly, 'while, you, Fanny, can tidy up this place. It looks as though a typhoon has swept through it. I will put the beds together when I can borrow the tools. Come along Ronald.'

He took my hand and I followed happily enough and we left Granny sighing heavily but getting down to sorting out their possessions, much as Mum would have to do when our trunks arrived, as she only had suitcases for the next week.

Grandpa was taller than me; he was sixty-seven with a head of thick white hair. The story went that he had been kicked by a horse at the age of twenty-one and went white overnight. I was not so sure. He had worked for years in China as an electrical engineer and Lloyd's surveyor, and having spent most of his working life in north China he could not imagine life anywhere else. The upheavals of the last three years had hit him very hard, literally turning his world upside down. Leaving his Tianjin home in Meadows Road after nearly a quarter of a century had affected him deeply. However, to me he was the same as I had always known him and I skipped along happily as he took me walking through the camp that was to be home for the next two and a half years, although I did not know it at the time.

We walked along the front of the rooms that were in their block, through an open kind of arch, although it looked as though there had once been a door. In front, running left to right, was the Rocky Road that Granny and I had walked along, turning left past Kitchen No. 1 on the right. This area, Blocks 1 to 15, had originally been for those who had come from Beijing and Qingdao, but Granny and Grandpa had been put into that area, and hence they were allocated Kitchen No. 1. After we walked about 150 yards we came to a playing field, three-quarters the size of a normal soccer pitch, marked out as a hockey field with a 'D' shaped penalty area. There was also a softball square in the south-east corner.

'Nearly all sports are played here. They had to restrict themselves to a softball diamond because someone worked out that if they played baseball the ball would forever be hit over the wall,' Grandpa added in explanation.

We turned right and walked past the Church. Grandpa went on to say, 'The Church is used by all Christian denominations. I think at the moment there are about 250 Roman Catholic priests in camp and nearly the same number of nuns, which with the Catholic congregation makes about 600 Catholics. Then there are about 600 Anglicans and 900 other Protestants.'

'That is about 2,100' I said, doing some rapid mental

arithmetic. I had been brought up to learn up to the 12 times table and been encouraged to repeat it almost daily, so juggling figures was never a chore.

'Yes, so you see that if all go to church there have to be services each hour of daylight on Sundays. Which to my mind is a good thing, because sermons have to be of the seven-minute variety. And in a way the clergy are quite happy in these difficult times, as more turn out than usual for the services.'

Just past the Church was Main Street, and as we crossed it I could see the guardroom on the right and the closed gates that we had come through when we had arrived down the hill to the left. Although that was only yesterday it seemed as though it lay somewhere in the distant past. In front of us was Number 3 Kitchen and some rooms backed up against the outside wall; these seemed to have been accommodation allocated to missionaries who had been at isolated mission stations.

The first buildings were the camp offices and the Commandant's Office. Grandpa hurried through these. I somehow felt that Grandpa was frightened to be seen by a Committee member and hauled in to do a job, which he was a few weeks later when he was roped in to sort out the electricity distribution. Grandpa did point out the post box and said that the Japanese allowed letters to places in China using the Chinese postal system, but they had to be addressed in Chinese characters. However, letters to England and America had to be written on Red Cross forms and placed in the box in the office for censorship.

Then past some more accommodation used by Catholic priests from the towns and cities in the hinterland of China. The camp wall continued with another watchtower and I saw a guard at the top carrying a rifle. Opposite, well within the camp was the 'Sunnyside Hospital', which had been built in the past twenty years. It was three stories in the front but having been built on a semi-cliff, as the ground dipped down to the river, the back was only two stories.

'Grandpa. Why is what you have called the hospital in such a dirty state?' I asked.

'The building was gutted and looted in the fighting between the Japanese and Chinese in 1937–8. Sadly most if not all the patients were bayoneted. That has been cleared up but the electric wiring and plumbing was all ripped out; it will take a lot of work before it can be used again as a hospital, although the top floor has been appropriated by Catholic priests for living accommodation. I suspect that you can see the fields from their windows, as the priests have devised a means of signalling to Chinese outside the camp. You can see that all the medicine has been poured away and pills are ground into the floors. Just wanton destruction.'

'What is "wanton" Grandpa?'

'It means needless, unnecessary.'

As we climbed up the slope of the ground, Grandpa added: 'You can see a couple of tennis courts and a basketball field. I suspect that was devised by the American Missionary Doctors to get patients to recover with exercise. Whilst basketball can be quite lively a game it can also be quite gentle. Americans are very keen on it.'

'Did you play basketball, Grandpa?'

'No,' he replied, laughingly, 'I am too short. One needs to be well over 6 foot to play properly. Even your Dad at over 6 foot did not, he concentrated on rugger, ice hockey, and recreational tennis with your mother.'

By now we had come to a little doorway, going through it there was a small field edged with trees. This seemed to have been taken over by Catholic priests, who were walking to and fro reading from their prayer books. I realised that they were saying their 'Office'. It was a poor substitute for cloisters, but better than nothing. There was another doorway in the corner and this led to a sort of passageway between the wall that separated the internees' part of the camp from the comfortable-looking, two-storey Japanese quarters, originally the Missionaries' Houses. The right wall just split off some more accommodation and a small field which I could see had mulberry trees. I recognised these from Beidaihe, and I knew that their berries were delicious and that the trees were ones you could climb. The rather useless acacias had very brittle branches, as I had found to my cost the last year in Beidaihe when a four-inch branch had snapped under my weight. I had been warned by Art, but in my usual manner of disregarding elder cousins like adults I had to find out for myself, fortunately with no broken bones. The acacias in Weihsien I identified as being too tall and thus unsafe, higher than about 12 feet.

'As we are now quite close to your room I will take you back to your parents,' Grandpa said, as I recognised the back of Kitchen No. 2.

Roger was playing in the dirt outside our door with some coloured wooden blocks that had been packed for him in my case. I squatted beside him, as he had also been given my 'official' toy, a metal ambulance about 12 inches long. I don't think that Mum had found my toy soldiers which I had smuggled on to the train, and still had. Then Grandpa went inside to speak to Mum.

***

The first few weeks we lived in Weihsien was a period of adjustment for everyone. I ran around freely with little parental supervision and played with the children living in and around the neighbouring blocks; in fact those first three months I tended not to wander too much from our room. The organising of schools was put into the 'difficult' tray, it was going to be too hot and there was no obvious building to use.

In normal times the next term would not have started until September, and anyway things might be different then. Our parents had a far worse time of it, trying to get accustomed to life in such restricted confines. In fact the room that we lived in seemed smaller than the enormous cupboard in which Mum had kept her clothes in Tianjin. Until our heavy baggage arrived we had to sleep on the floor, but fortunately Mum was able to borrow a cot, brought in by an expectant Mum who would not need it for a few months. That stopped Roger waking and grizzling on and off during the night. Otherwise I enjoyed sleeping on the floor, especially as I could keep my clothes on.

It was difficult trying to keep Roger clean; Mum washed his nappies, but I was left to my own devices. All the adults had had their luxury lifestyles abruptly terminated. The ladies suffered much more, doing their own chores. They had always been spoiled, with servants to do the domestic work.

In about ten days our trunks and beds arrived, dumped on the road near Kitchen No. 2. There was a general feeling of 'I'll help you if you will help me,' and the items got put on the ground in front of each room. The trunks had been broken into, but as they were mostly clothes nothing much had been taken.

The beds were intact but three full-sized beds and a cot would take more floor room than our room possessed. My parents realised that the only solution was bunks. The packing cases had to stay on the ground until they were dismantled, and the beds assembled. That was not an easy process as the door was too narrow to take an assembled bed unless turned on its side! Borrowing a claw hammer, Dad was able to retrieve the nails from our crates and straighten them on a stone.

Then Dad needed to borrow a saw. Our next door neighbours were Dr 'JW' Grice, his wife and their daughter Susie, who was about three years older than I. Dr Grice offered a saw but Dad declined on the grounds that 'It might be needed to take a leg off someone.' Dr Grice was the family GP in Tianjin and 'JW' and Kay Grice were good friends of my parents; he had been a British Army doctor during the First World War and sometimes could be persuaded to talk about the Mesopotamian campaign. However, in Rooms 2 and 3 of our block were the Dunjishahs. There were three daughters, Thritie, Katie and Frennie. Thritie was a bit older than I, Katie six months younger and Frennie two years younger. Mr Dhunjishah, who had been manager of the Talati House Hotel, had a complete carpenter's tool box, and Dad had no qualms borrowing his saw for the morning to cut up crates to make the beds into bunks. Dad opted for a top bunk with one below for Mum, her back still troubling her, whilst Roger and his borrowed cot had to stay on the floor. Thus I was made an upper bunk with long legs so that the space below could be used as well for the pram. I was always dubious at the stability of the arrangement, but did not fall out and it did not collapse.

It was right across camp to Block 7 where the men's showers were. When to go and have a shower was decided by Mum, when she often issued a tiny square of soap. My reaction to start with was 'Why can't I use the women's as they are much closer?' I was firmly rebuked for that thought and told that I was too old. Dad cut in to say he was going to the shower block and that I could come too. The shower block had a water tank built on a tower with a pump at the bottom, which was manually pumped by sixteen- to nineteen-year-old boys, so that the tank was filled and the water pressure gave what was considered a decent shower. When I first tried them I discovered that the water was 'cold only', too uncomfortable and as there was no other soap than a battered bit of carbolic which had been used by dozens, it seemed better to stay dry, unwashed but comfortable.

I also sneaked into the men's lavatories near the playing field when caught with the need, the urinals there basic but useable. One day I heard Mum having a whispered exchange with Dad on the subject, and he had told her quietly 'Don't let him go there, Margot, he can use your jerry in the hut here for the time being. The nearest "gents" are just not suitable for youngsters yet.'

Naturally this aroused my curiosity, and as soon as I could get away from my parents I did so. I recruited my new Weihsien friend, Joe Wilson, who lived in Block 41 Room 1, across the path from us but in the same compound. Joe was eighteen months younger, but nonetheless someone to play with. Anyhow, we found our way to the men's toilet block near the end of Block 23. It smelt pretty unpleasant as we approached and on entering found out why. There were no toilet units or seats, just shallow square cement 'basins' with two raised foot plates each side of a hole in the middle. There was no cistern and the means of flushing was a bucket which was filled under a pathetic tap in the far end. The whole place was running with sewage and even we, scruffy schoolboys, were horrified. There was a man taking his trousers down balancing on the foot rests, trying desperately to keep his trousers out of the various liquids, he shouted at us to get out as we stood gaping, whilst he bent and tried to align himself with the hole in the floor. We fled giggling and took to doing what we had to do against the toilet block wall, having made sure we were not seen. As to my father's edict I had no intention of using a potty, which I considered was for babies only. Mum could make her own arrangements, but I was not going down that route.

'I do not know what the fuss is about, Joe,' I said, 'The facilities are no different to the ones we provide for the servants in Tianjin, although we do give them a short piece of hose with a working tap. Puzzles me, where do they keep the paper? It can't be in reach' I continued. And then changed the subject.

After a few weeks the loo problem was largely cured. Amongst the camp inmates there were engineers of every kind, architects, builders and designers, not to mention doctors and teachers. Some form of engineer rigged up a way to flush the formerly un-flushable and we were allowed permission to use the cleaned-up facilities, with the caveat being 'only when wearing shorts'. When I looked puzzled, Mum said, 'If you go in there and try and take long trousers down you will get them into the filth. And, you will then stink and I am not washing stinking trousers. You know there is no laundry. The Japanese had one about six miles away and people started sending sheets and towels, only to find that they came back both torn and dirtier than they went in, if they were indeed returned. So we ladies have decided to boycott the laundry until a better one is provided.'

During April and May us boys kept clear of the blackened rubbish tip, which was adjacent to Blocks 23 and 24 yet only just over the wall from Block 41; there were too many adults trying their hands at scrounging bits to salvage. This pile of partly burnt furniture and laboratory equipment I had first seen on my walk with Granny the day after we arrived. Joe and I with one or two others used to sift through the ash to see if we could find anything for us to play with. We had got the idea from adults who had salvaged half-burnt furniture and repaired it to make it useable. Dad had even used some of the wood to make the headboards of our bunk beds. The certainty, to us boys, was that you got filthy, but by then we had worked out that if you finished by five in the afternoon you could get down to the showers and have a near hot shower because the sun had heated the water in the tank. Leave it any later and the adults had used all the warm water.

Soap was still a problem but one could rub hard, which was the only solution Mum had to offer. What little soap she had she needed for Roger.

One day towards the end of April, after the adults had given up on the area and removed anything of use or value, we came across some shards of broken glass. Joe cut himself and yelled, but I was too busy digging out something much more interesting, something different from below the glass.

'Look what I've found,' I crowed in delight. 'I think it's an engine or something like that.'

'Does it work?' asked Brian Calvert seriously. 'I bet it doesn't work.' Brian was six months older than I but we had known each other for years. In fact the last birthday party that I had been to was his in Tianjin. He now lived in Block 17 on the opposite side of the camp.

I tried to run it along the ground without much success. 'No, not really but I can still use it with my ambulance. I think the model is some sort of steam engine.'

'What would they use those for in a laboratory?' Joe asked curiously. We had all been told to keep away from this part of the rubbish pile as there was a lot of glass from broken laboratory equipment.

'Maybe they did experiments with steam engines,' I suggested, not having much idea.

'Possibly, better than this book anyway,' Joe muttered. He had found a half-charred physics book and was trying to decipher the symbols and make sense of it.

I was admiring my new toy when I was pounced upon from behind and the engine snatched out of my hand by a larger boy whom I did not recognise, from yet another part of camp. A scuffle followed and we both fell into the bonfire ash whilst we wrestled for possession of the treasure. I won but not before I had got myself covered in dirt. When I got back to our room Mum was horrified, but I was triumphant, although battered.

'Look at you,' she cried. 'We have very little soap and I have to wash everything by hand on a washboard in the washhouse. Roger's nappies take a lot of time and precious soap. How could you get so dirty? You are not to go and play near that bonfire again.'

Unfortunately, Dad backed Mum up, although I think that he thought it was quite amusing when I explained indignantly that I had only fallen in the ash because a bigger boy had tried to steal my trophy. But the ash pile was out of bounds at least for a few days, until my parents forgot about the incident.

Joe and I moved our operations to another part of the camp, nearer a kitchen where we could smell food even if we could not have it. One day we found a paper sack of very light grey powder, slightly torn but discarded behind a building near some low bushes, and smuggled it back to Blocks 41 and 42. We got some water and found that if mixed with earth it made perfect modelling clay which was quite hard when dry. We spent a whole day making several masterpieces.

A couple of days later we were found by an American man, who at first admired our efforts, then got rather upset when he read the label on the bag. 'Hey kids, this stuff is cement,' he told us so loudly that several other men were attracted to the scene. 'What the hell are you doing playing with this? We can use this for building. You had no right to mess with this.'

'Did you split open this bag?' demanded another man who had come up. 'If so, you should have your backsides tanned.' We shook our heads guiltily and decided to retreat urgently before any more trouble occurred.

Sadly, I got into another row back at our room. Mum had hardly got over the ash affair, as she called it, and now here I was covered in grey sticky stuff and mud that was all in my hair. She was furious and complained that wild kids like me would make life unbearable in a very short space of time.

Other mothers must have had similar experiences; with the walls joining the blocks and making the camp into a series of little compounds it was difficult to see what was going on. Thus, in early May they decided that organising the children into some sort of school to occupy them, particularly the boys, was essential, if only for the adults' sanity.

There were about 200 children out of around 2,000 inmates, mostly English and American. The only spare area was in front of the hospital, the bottom two floors, which were being renovated. Our first teacher was a nun who got us to sit down, but as we had no paper we were taught algebra by drawing equations in the sandy ground. The children from twelve to fifteen were worked harder, but they did get scraps of paper to write on. Over sixteen had to work around the camp as the men and some women did.

The brakes had been put on running wild, hopefully not for long.

As the weather grew hotter all lessons were taught outside, often sitting under the trees. Then we had a harridan of a teacher, Miss Rudd, who had a shock of snow-white hair, was slightly lame and used a walking stick. One could not get away from her, as she had the knack of flicking her stick to hold the ferrule end and then catch your ankle with the curved handle. Anyhow she started us on Latin verbs. I got quite used to etching the ground with a stick with 'Amo, Amas, Amat...' but somehow it did not hold my interest as sums did.

By late May all the leaves were out on the trees and us nine- to eleven-year-olds were detailed to collect leaves from each of the different trees. There were over 100 types and I collected nearly that number. These were the trees that had been planted to assist in the long-forgotten mission schools' botany classes. They also served to make a great contrast to the treeless plain outside the camp. In the trees were also a lot of birds, including the golden oriole. Thinking ahead I could see another teacher, another day, saying '...and please collect as many different bird feathers as you can.'

The teachers felt that they had to encourage us and devised small prizes. Someone had realised that the odd food parcel from friends and later the Red Cross parcels contained a bar of chocolate. Most bars would break into ten squares, and a square of chocolate was a wonderful prize for a ten-year-old. A policy with which I heartily agreed. Especially as I was usually the winner.

Once the commandant saw that the children were under some sort of control, he gave orders for paper and pencils to be made available. Drawing was then encouraged and art teachers came out of the woodwork. There were rules, though. The Japanese would not allow anything to be drawn of the outside of the camp. Drawing of the watchtowers or of the guards was forbidden. We could draw only trees, bushes and birds in the middle of the camp; we would draw portraits, but nothing of military value. I was never very good with the birds, flowers or the bees but quite tolerable on buildings and perspective.

In late June the expected baby arrived, but was born with a cleft palate and lip. To the limited surgical means available in Weihsien Camp Hospital this presented a serious problem. Fortunately, the inmates included Dr Harold Louks, an American surgeon who had practised 'plastic' surgery at Peking's Yenching University Hospital, which was where he had been captured. There was also Dr Grice, our British GP and surgeon from Tianjin. Dr Grice lived in the next room to ours in Block 42, and after the birth came to me and said, 'There is a little baby girl who has just been born and is very sick and cannot eat and I would like some of your toy soldiers to make her better.'

I looked at my precious toys and asked wistfully if it mattered if the doctor took ones which had had their head or arms broken off, and was relieved to find that Dr Grice was quite happy with the broken ones as he was going to melt them anyway. The broken lead toy soldiers were duly taken to the camp hospital where they were melted and moulded to form an artificial palate and sewn into the roof of the baby's mouth.[53] Susan Dobson made a full recovery and I caught up with her as recently as 2005, when I learnt that from Weihsien she had gone to London and had a more conventional palate sewn in her mouth, in a well-known children's hospital.

Meanwhile, on 29th June 1943, there had been a death in the hospital, a Dutch priest who had been admitted to hospital, almost as soon as he arrived in Weihsien, with typhoid. He was not very old, in his sixties, I was told, but that still seemed ancient to me. The funeral was held a couple of days after the death. The whole camp attended the funeral or watched it. After the service in the Church, the coffin was carried out by six priests all of about the same height. The procession started with all the RC priests in their vestments, the nuns in their habits and all the Anglican and Protestant clergy in either vestments or best suits, as the internees of all denominations then filed in after the principal mourners. In the end there was probably a total of 800 in the procession, headed by five RC Bishops, an Abbot, an Anglican Bishop and the senior American Presbyterian Preacher, all singing suitable hymns to the tunes of the Salvation Army Band. This was reinforced with three or four priests in soutanes blowing trumpets or trombones, as well as Jonesy Jones, Wayne Adams and Pineapple Alama, the three dance band musicians whose tour of the Far East had been rudely short-ened when the war broke out. I was very much a spectator to start with, but then I saw Susie Grice, our neighbour, walking and joined the procession myself. Very impressive, to a nine-year-old.

But, I thought, 'Why does it take a tragedy to get them all together?' I knew that some of the participants would not pass the time of day, let alone a religious ceremony, with each other in different circumstances.

The procession ended at the graveyard, which was in the south-east corner of the Japanese area, somewhere we would not, under normal circumstances, be allowed to enter, but on this occasion the guards stood back, saluted the coffin and held the gates open for the mourners.

After the burial proper, I thought this was an ideal time to investigate the layout of this prohibited area of camp, so I took my time making my way back. The reconnaissance was later to prove useful.

Then in July the Japanese, who disliked gatherings of adults and children, stopped our lessons, fearing they were in preparation for some kind of organised disturbance. I was very happy to go back to running wild throughout the camp, now I knew my way around and was a wiser boy after two months self-education. But the adults soon got weary of mobs of uncontrolled children and petitioned to allow Scouts, Guides, Brownies and Cubs to be formed. Rather surprisingly this was granted, on condition that their activities mainly took place in the South Field. There was an ample number of people who had been Scoutmasters, or in the case of the younger priests remembered being Rover Scouts. I had an advantage in that I had my own copy of the handbook, which I guarded carefully. We had no uniforms, but the ladies looked around at their hoarded 'might be useful things' for felt to embroider badges, which we wore on our ordinary clothes. The pattern could not be the same as Baden-Powell had designed, but our 'Cub' badges ended up eight-sided with 'Weihsien'. The Japanese thought this a marvellous idea and provided the lone occasion when an outside photographer was allowed in to take 'team type' photographs, so that the Japanese could show the world that they were treating Allied internees correctly. Dad helped to set up the Scouts with Mr O'Hara; both had been in Tianjin, where they had been respectively Deputy and Head Commissioner of Scouts for North China before the war. Mr Kerridge, another pre-war Scoutmaster, often gathered us in groups under the plane trees, which were planted five foot or so in from the walls of the Field. The Scout movement failed by the winter as there were suddenly a lot more children and there was no adequate accommodation to protect meetings from the cold weather.

When the school started again in September the question

of 'where' raised its head. The hospital was a proper hospital now and an alternative venue was needed. As the Church was only occupied on Sundays it was deemed that the Church pews would be suitable. So I started again under Miss Rudd, who retained her ability to trip one up with her walking stick, but had now added the ability to lift one up by the hair if one was being exceptionally thick, or obstructive. Each class was allocated two rows of pews with two more rows between each class. It just did not work, as we told the officiating adults, but the views of young boys that run contrary to those of adults are generally discarded. The noise of voices went down to the altar, whilst the voice of the preacher went up to the back. Teachers working at one end of the pews could not be heard at the other end. That experiment lasted three weeks before it was officially accepted that it was bedlam and declared, 'Good idea but failed.' Thus us kids were back on the 'streets' again.

But before the Church School idea had happened, sports had started to be organised by everyone. Softball was played by most. The Catholic priests fielded several teams, some of which were very good, probably as they were Americans and had been playing softball all their lives. The remaining nuns formed another team. The adults and children over twelve played theirs in the big field near to the Church, whilst those younger played in the small South Field.

We also invented a game generally played in the light summer evenings on the main sports field: two teams were chosen and each team had a 'home' in the penalty 'D' of the hockey markings. The idea was to get 'home' while the opposite team had to try and stop you, and if they did you were taken back as a prisoner and had to hold on to the previous prisoner. If one of your own team cut the prisoners' line all those freed prisoners started again. It occupied us all for a couple of hours, made sure we were tired when we went to bed, and in spite of fights, arguments and occasional cheating we enjoyed the diversion very much.

One thing that most of the families did was to subscribe to the *Peking Chronicle*, an English-language newspaper printed in Beijing, and edited by a German editorial team. Reading it through one could estimate the progress of the war. It, however, had a far more essential function when torn into small squares – toilet paper was as ever in short supply. Us boys often did not have the time or inclination to go back to our huts to get some and, while definitely avoiding stinging nettles, tended to use softish leaves, equally good to our minds.

7

Catering and its Absence

Filling my stomach was probably the single most important event in each and every day. I was young and growing and always hungry. I had been spoiled in Tianjin, we had employed a cook, and he was good. I relished his speciality, which was to make a duck and two-chicken roast, although a pheasant often replaced the second chicken in the winter. He used to bone them whole and put one inside another and then use stuffing to put them into shape, so that then when it came to carving a knife would glide through the lot.

Dad and his brother Harold used to go shooting in the spring or late autumn and other than pheasant they shot snipe and mallard. However, when the latter was served I had got used to asking if it was walkie-walkie duck or flying duck. The snipe I considered a waste of time because you needed a lot of patience to carve out a fork-full. The previous six months, when we had been living in those two rooms at the Talati House Hotel in Tianjin, we had still enjoyed plenty to eat. There was no real shortage then, as the Chinese peasant farmers still brought their produce to the old British covered market in Dagu Lu (Dagu Road). This had been built by the Administrators of the British Concession probably thirty years before. Two things were different from markets in the 21st century: there was no refrigeration, hence fish were kept alive in large tanks of water. And poultry was also kept alive; this was to prevent unscrupulous traders plumping up the body with a hypodermic needle of water. The odd time that I had visited the market it was an education, seeing the various cooks selecting the ingredients by feeling the live flesh to make certain that they were not being duped. Tianjin, before we left, had not changed. But Weihsien was completely different. There really was a war on and we were almost in the middle of it.

In the first weeks I remember little of our precise diet, except that we ate a lot of bread produced by Qingdao Bakery, and not a lot else. This arrangement could only last for a few months, after which the inmates would be on their own. A Greek baker, Mr Stephanides from Qingdao, had brought in some yeast and was appointed camp baker, and I suppose he was multiplying the yeast. All food had to be made by the inmates themselves, but since the adults had all employed cooks pre-war they did not even have latent skills on which to call. The bread was rather lead-like at first, but soon the bakers got accustomed to the quantities to use, and the fact that yeast needed sugar to rise properly was 'discovered', not that much sugar was ever available. The task was fairly formidable: 400 loaves a day were needed to feed 2,000 people.

As food was precious, as much as possible was done to minimise waste. Thus any stale bread was boiled up as porridge for the next breakfast. The experience has left me with a lifelong dislike for bread sauce. We did have flour, which

81

was so different from other Japanese camps in Shanghai, Hong Kong and Singapore, where the staple was rice and with it vitamin B deficiency for the consumers. The flour supplied slowly deteriorated as the years passed, until by the end it was mostly weevils' bodies – protein I suppose – and millet seeds that were milled, but which in their natural state looked remarkably like the seeds that one buys in bags to feed wild birds today.

My mother brought all our rations back from the kitchen to our room and we always ate there at a folding games table that came in our luggage. She did not want us to eat in the crowded dining room, and most other families with children under five did the same. The queues for serving and eating would have been impossible otherwise, and bawling two-year-olds would have added nothing but irritation to the atmosphere.

The camp had a policy at the kitchens that, if you ate in the dining room, you could ask for a second helping, not always forthcoming, but over the months 'Seconds' became almost universally used as a description for more. Manuel Sotolongo, an eight-year-old Cuban, caused a big laugh when he asked for seconds of salt, pepper and mustard.

I knew very little about the workings of the kitchens, as children were prohibited to go in them. I did take a peek a few times. They were hot, with open fires, with a decking over in which up to five large 'woks' or 'Kongs' were set. These were about five feet across (1½ metres) with a wooden lid, used to boil water and make stew. (Recipe: water, lots of vegetables and an occasional cube of meat.) Often one of the men had to balance precariously over the lid to retrieve something and it was also not unknown for the lid to collapse and the volunteer cook then got scalded legs. The cooks did make tempting smells with their soups and stews.

Sadly, lack of supplies meant second helpings were few and one had to be satisfied with the aroma.

These thin stews were generally our daily fare for at least one meal. I did not think too much of them: the meat, if you could find it, was stringy, the vegetables over-cooked, even if they were often soya beans or soya bean leaves, and almost a mush. I also missed having any milk to drink. The alternative was water, and even that was a problem as the shallow wells were only five metres from the cesspits. Mum felt that water should be boiled – definitely a desirable policy – but most of the time there was no fuel, so that was but seldom implemented.

There were three cows grazing in the graveyard in the Japanese area of camp. Pathetic beasts, which were milked for the babies and the hospital patients. Roger had a cupful on most days; I eyed it once and it had been so watered down that the milk took on a bluish tinge. I decided I was not missing very much.

Mum said that we had not brought in much in the way of food, although this puzzled me as Roger's Pedigree pram had been overloaded with the stuff. I think really Mum was of the opinion that it was better to use currently issued supplies and keep the tins 'in case', for the future.

Thus, like a lot of families, my parents patronised the small canteen provided by the Japanese to buy extras. The canteen was staffed by inmates, supplying, when they had such goods, cigarettes, toilet paper and sometimes small quantities of soap, peanut oil, dried fruit and spices. But we had to have ration cards for these sorts of items and the card had to be marked. They were paid for by money that inmates were given, called 'comfort money'. It was supplied by the British Government to the Swiss, whose Consul in Qingdao, Mr Eggers, used to make a monthly visit starting with a suitcase full of Chinese dollars. I never had much to do with money and the lack of it made little difference to me, in any case the management of any money was in the hands of my mother. But I did notice that Mum's small trinkets seemed to disappear from time to time. I learned these financed extra food like eggs for us from the black market.

Anyone who was around ten years old knew that a big trade was happening over the wall, mainly in food, though nobody ever said anything. Watching and sometimes getting involved, even if inadvertently, was fascinating. The main organiser of the black market was an Australian Cistercian Monk, Fr Patrick Scanlan, using priests to make the transactions. There was a general curfew at lights out, 10 p.m., but in the summer evenings it was not unusual for us boys to sneak out of bed and see what was going on, usually as a sort of dare.

We soon spotted the priests trading over the walls, but nobody ever betrayed them, even to our parents, although I knew from Mum that she was grateful for those extras, even though she was not sure precisely how it was done. Order placed one night, eggs or whatever received the next.

But rapidly the guards realised what was going on and more devious methods had to be introduced, especially when they started cocking their rifles and firing the odd shot in the air. The standard of trust was sufficiently low that it was jewellery, or money, up front.

Fr Scanlan, realising that inmates were free to practice their religion, instigated a system whereby the priests would walk around the hospital area holding their breviaries, but also bearing a basket, hung on a belt under their soutanes. The basket started out being filled with money and sometimes jewellery; towards the end, after the transactions, it now contained the food of various sorts that was on order. One of the older priests had difficulty walking, and had asked his Bishop if he could say his office seated against the wall, and we boys often used to sit by the wall with him idly talking. I was doing that one evening with Brian just after supper. Two guards approached the priest, speaking broken English, and said that there was no way he could read in that light.

The priest said, 'I have very good eyes I can read clearly,' I suspected that the guards had thought the breviary was a diversion. So they then said 'Then read to us.'

The priest then started *'Pater noster, qui es in caelis Sanctificetur nomen tuum…'* I had difficulty stopping from bursting out laughing, because it was obvious the light was too bad to read and the recitation was from memory. But it satisfied the guards and they left. Brian and I then said goodnight and we both got up off the ground to leave, but the priest said, 'Boys, would you mind taking these to Fr Scanlan,' producing two boxes of eggs from under his soutane!

One evening in July Dad came in from his job as a stoker in Kitchen No. 2 to relax before our last meal of the day. 'The Trappist, Fr Scanlan, who smuggles over the wall has been caught by the Japs,' he told Mum.

'How did that happen?' she asked, obviously shocked. 'What will happen to him now?'

Dad shrugged his shoulders. 'The Japs are going to try him, so it seems.'

The whole camp was aware of the coming trial and it wasn't just his fellow clergy who were praying that the Japanese would not decide to make an example of the monk. I did not consider it myself, but Mum admitted that many of the adults were afraid he would be executed. He was tried by the Japanese Consular Police, and the only internee allowed at the proceedings was Ted McClaren, the 'head' of the internees. The sentence was one month in solitary confinement. I heard some adults saying that was a fitting penance for an Australian Trappist monk.

Then the Japanese had a problem. The Commandant's House was the northernmost of the old missionary houses and the nearest to the internee section of the camp. The only cell was on the ground level of his house. Because of the construction of the houses, the top two floors were living accommodation, whereas the ground level was rather like a cellar and used as such. Fr Scanlan was duly placed in the cell and allowed his breviary. But then Fr Scanlan hit back: he had a fine voice, and used it to sing the 'office' in plainsong. Fr Scanlan's fellow priests got as near as they could in a narrow path between two walls and either responded to Fr Scanlan's chanting or all recited the office out loud. The Japanese listened appreciatively, although the latter was unintelligible to them. They were still relatively relaxed when the midnight office was sung, but come 3 a.m. they were woken up and were displeased. This procedure lasted for a few days. After a week Fr Scanlan was escorted in front of the Commandant again, in the presence of Ted McClaren, to be told that for good behaviour he was being released. Facesaving by the Japanese, as they would not of course admit that it was Fr Scanlan's voice at 3 a.m. that had driven them crazy, and they had to put a stop to it somehow.

Peanuts came over the wall in great quantity, and peanut butter became a staple to be put on bread. Ordinary mincing machines were modified by replacing the single cutter and fitting a pair which ground the peanuts into a paste. The rather tedious task of winding the mincing machine on the table usually fell to me. I did this chore for our immediate family and for others in Block 42, always ensuring they got the same amount of peanuts back.

The priests really impressed me in Weihsien; they had become the unofficial morale leaders. Many had long black beards, which I guessed were why my parents had called them 'Daddy Whiskers' in the past. I had occasionally been taken to All Saints Anglican Church in Tianjin, the Church my parents were married in, and they did not go too often in Weihsien. Mum always used Roger as an excuse, saying that he would probably bawl and disturb the service. Dad was into 'bells and smells', I think from his time at Abbotsholme.[54] I was not bound to go regularly, but I found solace in going to sit on the wall near the Church during Roman Catholic Mass and listening to the chanting of plainsong. It was an experience I always enjoyed, although I could not read a note of music at the time. I liked classical music but I think that I inherited my tone-deaf voice from Mum. In fact, I am sure, because Dad could and often did play the piano in Tianjin.

Suddenly, on 8th August 1943, an announcement was made that the priests and nuns were being moved to Beijing, as a result of a request from the Pope. They had one week in which to pack up, and half were to leave on 16th August and the other half a week later. It was with great sadness that we saw them go. The Bishops had agreed for about half a dozen priests and the same number of nuns to stay at Weihsien to administer to the needs of the Catholic community. Fr Rutherford, an American Franciscan and a great softball player despite his girth, who was staying behind, told me that those that were being moved to Beijing were going to be farmed out amongst the various monasteries or convents in the Beijing area and would no longer be fed by the Japanese. Their accommodation and rations would have to be provided by the Church, but they would still be subject to curfew, and their movements restricted.

Magically, there was now space in the camp and plans were being made for a proper school.

8

The Inmates Change

The departure of over a quarter of the inmates to Beijing should have meant that their rooms became free, so Dad went along to the office in the hopes that he could get a second room for us. Tom Waters apparently told Dad that he had been informed by the Commandant that there were to be further big changes in the list of inmates soon, but as yet no timescale was given. Tom was understandably reluctant to make major changes until he knew how many internees there were going to be.

On 9th September 1943 trucks came in the front gate bringing prospective internees. There were boys and girls, some younger than me, and a few teenagers, accompanied by adults: all in all a total of 200. We soon learnt that they were members and staff from the China Inland Mission School at Chefoo.[55] They had previously been confined to the school premises, Temple Hill, Yantai (Chefoo), and had left Chefoo a couple of days earlier by tramp steamer to sail round the coast to Qingdao, and then a four-hour train journey to Weihsien. The schoolchildren were moved into Blocks 23 and 24, just vacated by the nuns. The married teachers, especially those with children, were allocated hut rooms rather like ours.

The camp inmates were called together a couple of days later on the big sports field. The Commandant through his interpreter announced that there would be another change of personnel. The American and Canadian governments had identified some 2,000 Japanese who were living in their countries, and Japan would exchange them with 2,000 people that were in various Japanese Civilian Assembly Centres. The names of the lucky ones from Weihsien would be read out, and they would be leaving in three days. They were to travel to Shanghai, where they would get on a Japanese ship to be taken to the Portuguese town of Goa in India, where the exchange would take place. A Swedish ship, the MV *Gripsholm*, would then take them on to New York. There was great rejoicing by all the Americans and Canadians present; the British remained glum. With the total reduction of 450 priests and nuns, who had already gone, and now 500 Americans and Canadians, Dad thought that the camp population would end up 1,100 British, and 200 other nationals, mainly Americans.

When we got back to our room, Mum said it was not fair, but Dad pointed out that it was an exchange and that there apparently were not enough Japanese living in the British Isles. It turned out later that the majority of the Japanese in the Commonwealth were to be found in Australia, and Australia would not let them be exchanged because most of them lived on the north-west coast between Darwin and Perth, with many pearl and oyster fishermen among their number. Their knowledge of the coast would be invaluable to the Japanese military in the event of an invasion of Australia.

The next day there was a knock on the door, and Tom Waters was greeted by Mum; I think Dad was out on his stoker's shift.

'Margot, I thought that I would pop in and say that, as a result of the toing and froing, I have got you down for Block 13 Rooms 10 and 11. Your parents are in Room 12, so you will have a babysitter. You should be able to move in three or four days.' Mum thanked him profusely.

Thus when Dad got home he was greeted by Mum with the words 'We have been moved to two rooms, next to Mother and Father. We have got a few days to do it. I suggest that after breakfast tomorrow, we go and see what state it's in. I believe that there was an American Missionary family in it.' Obviously Mum had made plans as to how the move might be managed.

So we duly trooped across to Block 13. The dividing walls for the courtyard were due to come down by the weekend, so we would not have a courtyard but rather a lot of bricks, though without cement. Otherwise, the new rooms were convenient as we had an internal door between the two rooms, so Mum decreed that they would have their outside door firmly locked and entry would be through the door of Roger's and my room. As she pointed out, one fewer door in use meant more hanging space.

The move went remarkably smoothly. Mr Dhunjishah gave Dad a hand to take down the bunk beds, and Grandpa was in his element supervising their re-construction. The trunks, beds and broken-down crates were pushed across in a rather larger cart by Dad. I was employed shuttling back and forth with Roger's pram: no Roger within, but rather our possessions, filled up on the way out, empty on the return to Block 42. Mum loaded at one end and Granny emptied at the other.

Winter was not far away. Most of the huts had no heating and those with experience of the climate estimated that the temperature could fall as low as 0°F, or minus 17°C. The

Japanese promised coal, thus each room needed a stove (the dormitory rooms already had pot-bellied iron stoves, fitted with chimneys made out of four-inch (10cm) tin tubing). The coal duly arrived: a couple of buckets of black powder with the odd walnut-sized lump. One could not burn it in the open and there were no hearths. So, from the engineers came a rapid design for those hut rooms without stoves. They were to build new ones: three foot long, built from bricks obtained from those demolished walls which had once defined each courtyard between the blocks. The stove included an oven, made from a square five-gallon oil tin, and a chimney built out of ¾-pint soup tins carefully pushed into each other. There was no solder, so the engineers stressed the need to ensure that the top of each tin went snugly into the one before, so that smoke could not leak into the room. Leakage of carbon monoxide, which came from incomplete burning of fuel, was potentially fatal: it could kill the occupants as they slept.[56]

The ovens meant that housewives could cook a little extra, if they could find ingredients. They certainly could keep food hot after collecting it from the kitchen. Often though, there was so little of the food that at any temperature it tasted great. The trouble with the 'private' stoves was fuel, and I recall seeing Mr Nathan, who was Chief General Manager of the Kailan Mining Administration, a man regarded with great respect and who was at least ten years older than Dad, atop the ash pile outside of No. 1 Kitchen. He was carrying a little bucket with him, and had climbed up there in order to pick up, very carefully, small pieces of partially burnt coal to take to his dormitory to burn in their stove. It seemed so ironic: here was a businessman used to dealing with thousands of tons of coal being forced by a war to try to find, with his bare hands, a couple of pounds for his own use.

The Japanese realised that all this illegal building of stoves was going on, and issued smaller cast iron stoves but without the chimney piping. And policy caught up with the facts: you needed to have been issued a stove to be allowed to draw coal, so Dad got two, one for each room. He then had a brilliant idea when he saw the unscrewed top of the pot-bellied stove – he promptly mounted it on the bricks so that there was now a 'ring' to heat kettles and saucepans, and the oven for the 'brick' stove.

Dad said, 'I have already scrounged a five-gallon oil tin, and I must now find enough soup, fruit or vegetable tins to make the chimney. I have staked a claim for a number of bricks from one of the end walls. I have also got a small bag of that cement you were playing with ages ago, Ronald, which when mixed with mud should do to cement the bricks together and seal the top.'

When challenged, I agreed that I had a number of iron bars that would make a grate, again trophies from the fire and ash pile from what seemed months before. 'I told you Mum, that they would come in useful.' Mum had to agree that one could ever tell when things would find a purpose. That was the first and only agreement that I ever had from Mum regarding my trait of squirreling things away 'in case' they might be wanted. I had pointed out to her that she herself was keeping all those tins of food that had been so elaborately brought in Roger's pram for a 'rainy day'.

Then we were told that we were being given new internee numbers to wear, and we had to collect new three-by-four-inch cloth name badges, to be on display at all times. The number consisted of one's group number, a number up to fifteen, and an individual number to aid counting. We were lined up each morning in sequence in each group, although on occasions we had a 'grand' roll call on the sports field, when the group number became the row number. I always eyed the watchtower with its machine gun that I had seen on my very first evening at Weihsien. During roll call it was not unknown for us boys, having been counted once, to run behind the backs of the adults to be counted again, which when it occurred totally confused the guards and caused much scratching of heads. The adult internees did not take kindly to such antics because it often lengthened roll call to a couple of hours, and the guards took it out on the adults, slapping their faces, while I among the other boys got away scot-free.

By now the teaching staff of the Chefoo School had got themselves organised. They decreed that as they were an intact complete boarding school, and that they, the teachers, were responsible for other people's children, Chefoo School should try to continue as it had before in Yantai. And, as before, there would be no fraternisation with children of 'commercial' parents – social classes would be kept separate. To a large extent this was already the de facto position: the Chefoo scholars had been strutting around as though they owned the world. An attitude that did not settle well with those who had been in Weihsien six months longer.

Grubby fists came into play, and the missionary children were taught the facts, but this of course drove them into the hands of their teachers, who were the instigators of the 'separation' in the first place. The only exception would be on the sports field, with supervised games. This policy was imposed strictly by Chefoo schoolteachers. I frankly thought that they were being idiotic, but gradually the real reason behind it all emerged: the Chefoo teachers felt that schools like Tianjin Grammar School and Beijing American School had too many Catholics, and even people of mixed race, and that the purity of their Protestant charges was endangered.

I always found this attitude difficult to understand, because they were forever emphasising that they were missionary teachers, loving everyone. Like all stupid policies it would not last and was finally overturned eighteen months later.

More immediately, and after we had digested the school division policy, a couple of days later, at supper, Dad said that he had now finished the stove but that we would need fuel to burn in it. Dad was still working as a kitchen stoker, but with the move to Block 13 he had been transferred to No. 1 Kitchen, across the rocky road from our new block, but a bit further north.

'There is nothing for it Ronald,' said Dad, 'you will have to make coal balls as the coal we are to be given for burning is literally dust. I know, as I am having to try and burn it in Kitchen 1. Dad was having some success, which he attributed to the fact that they had bigger fireplaces there, under the kitchen Kongs.

So, after asking around, I started my new job. The coal ball recipe was 60 per cent coal dust and 40 per cent mud, with enough water to make a really thick paste. You had to take a handful and using both hands mould it like a small snow-ball. Then you placed it on the ground to dry. If you really wanted one to burn quicker add 10% sawdust. That was the easy part; getting the residue off your hands and arms was a different matter. Soap was in short supply and hard to get hold of. My suggestion to Mum that I be allowed to help do the clothes washing fell on stony ground. It was a huge concession by me, as I had never thought much of soap, and only used it in the past under the direct persuasion of Funainai.

'You are not coming near to the washing with those hands – find a bucket of water and scrub!'

After a couple of times with this method, Grandpa came

to the rescue. 'Ronald, I've got a half-sized tin, which used to have salmon or fish in it. With a couple of nails we can fix it to a piece of wood, and then with another piece of wood you can fill the tin, press the coal mixture down hard and then, if you bang it on a brick, you will get a perfectly round, if flattened, coalball.' This I tried and found that it worked, and so from then on I got less black dust under my fingernails. The semi-mechanised coal-ball production got into its stride and continued intermittently, whenever the weather turned cold.

By now Mum, who had always been an inveterate letter-writer, had established correspondence with my Aunt Freda, as well as Danish and French friends in Tianjin. In addition to guarded exchange of news, food parcels sometimes used to get through. Along with the little luxuries like tea and coffee, Mum found that the more substantial food like tinned corned beef had generally been 'liberated', probably when the parcels were inspected by 'Postal Customs'. Mum was still excused work, although come 8th October, which was Roger's second birthday, she started vegetable peeling and cooking in Kitchen No. 1, but on a different shift to Granny, so that one of them could look after Roger. These two somehow thickened our soups or stews heated up in the room stove by adding selected bits of vegetable peelings or soya beans. This policy did allow me free rein; I was no longer tied to Roger.

The way we boys played was very territorial, based either on the physical location of our rooms or the kitchen in which we ate. As I had changed kitchens and moved well away, I felt resignation from my first gang was a better way out than the inevitable eviction. I soon caught up with Michael and Peter Turner, twins from Tianjin, who had a young sister, Barbara, in Block 2. Their parents again were good friends with Mum and Dad. Brian Calvert used to join up with us on some days.[57]

In November came another chapter in the Chefoo School transfer, as half a dozen children were moved to one of the Shanghai Camps to be reunited with their parents. Then, finally, the following February, four more children, who had been caught in Shanghai, came the other way, to Weihsien, where their parents already were.

9

The First Weihsien Christmas

As boys we were always looking for a sport we could practise, and the latest phase was to tease the guards. One of their Sergeants, a big swarthy bloke for a Japanese, who used to wear a ridiculously small forage cap on a large shaven head, was often baited. He seemed to know only one phrase of Chinese – 'Bushinde' – which he would yell out at us; it meant 'Don't do that!' or 'You can't do that!' Very soon, whenever we saw him, we used to form a circle, out of arm's reach, and taunt him with the word before running off. At first he resented the nickname and would get furious. But after a while he seemed to accept it and almost liked it, I suspect. Another nickname was coined when an adult described a guard as King Kong, as he reminded her of the gorilla of that name in the 1930s film.

Not that taunting was restricted to harassing the guards. There was an American missionary family in Block 15 with three young children, and they would start the day rolling around on the dirt outside their rooms while saying their 'prayers'. This inevitably got around, so a bunch of us used to get there before breakfast and start rolling around in the mud mimicking them. They invoked the 'freedom of religion right', and six ten- or eleven-year-olds were duly paraded in front of the Committee and sentenced to be caned if we kept doing it. So that ended us baiting the 'Holy Rollers'.

Finding something to do that was acceptable was growing ever more difficult.

A month to go to Christmas. Mum sent off Christmas cards, which Dad had made with a hectograph,[58] which he had constructed using an old half-inch-deep baking dish. He copied the design on to pre-stamped post cards, which the Japan censor allowed.

Mum also went quite often across to our old block to talk to Mrs Grice, who had lived next door. The latter was a great fount of gossip and 'happenings' in the camp. Apparently the Belgian 'de Saint-Hubert' family of four were not liked as they cheated by stealing vegetables and coal and collected four portions from the kitchen hatch to take to their room in Block 33, having first had a meal in the Kitchen Dining area. A lady had challenged them and a fight ensued. So, all was not happy in the camp, and when you dug around the more disquiet you found.

Mum got back to say that Mrs Grice had mentioned that Susie had got some coloured paper, and suggested that I go across and help her make paper chains for Christmas decorations. That did not last long because we ran out of glue, and flour could not be spared to make any more. The adults had tried to make Christmas as normal as possible for those under fifteen, in the circumstances. I got a bar of chocolate, and a box of peanuts.

We collected our Christmas breakfast on Christmas Eve, sausages and an egg each. The sausages were either heavily seasoned or slightly off. Dad looked at them, pronounced that they were beef and took the view that if there was no mould on them they would be safe enough to eat if well cooked. Christmas breakfast was bread porridge, a sausage and a fried egg – sheer luxury. Another teaspoon of tea leaves was added to the pot to freshen up the taste. When the teapot was full of leaves, it was emptied and the cycle repeated.

The main Christmas meal was at lunchtime; somehow the Japanese had produced roast pork. The portions were small but tasty and with lots of vegetables. Christmas puddings rounded off the meal: everybody had donated some dried fruit and the cooking 'Kongs' were ideal to boil them in, wrapped in sheets. Before that people had been going round giving each other presents. A calendar here, a hand-made brooch there. I was quite content with my big bar of chocolate.

Then, on 28th December, each kitchen had a party for a group of children. No. 1 Kitchen's was for the nine- to twelve-year-olds. I met a few others, mostly girls, who were new to me. I could not see them wanting to climb walls or trees, or even play with soldiers.

The next day Fr Palmers, a Belgian priest, organised a concert during which it was announced that Blocks 43 and 44 had to be cleared and No. 3 Kitchen, up to now the 'Beijing Kitchen', closed with the users moved to No. 1 Kitchen, but any food supplies in the kitchen were to be left behind. The rumour was that more internees were due to arrive. The news spread like a forest fire, yet eavesdropping on the adults' talk made the mystery no clearer: nobody could think who they could be. Then, on New Year's Eve, sixty Italians arrived, some at breakfast time and some mid-morning, and were allocated Blocks 43 and 44 and No. 3 Kitchen. Mr Eggers, the Swiss Consul from Qingdao, came to ensure that they were allocated correctly and to record their names.

Most came from Shanghai, but there were half a dozen from Beijing and Tianjin. From them the camp learnt the latest war news, things like Italy had opted out of the war and the German Navy's *Scharnhorst* battleship had been sunk.

A friend of Mum's, Hilda Hale, who lived in Block 14, came round to say that she was abandoning her Black Market circle. Their two rooms had been searched minutely over the past couple of days, and as getting supplies over the wall was becoming very difficult with the lack of Catholic priests she had decided to pack it in. Mrs Lawless, who was in her fifties and lived next to her, had had her room literally turned out. Although Mrs Lawless was born Swiss, the Japanese seemed to have taken a severe dislike to them both. Hilda then went on to say that she was going to give her stock of 30 lbs of millet to Dr Grice for hospital patients.

Then Kay Grice arrived to collect some of the millet. Often, when three or more women end up in the same place, gossip begins. So, listening in to their conversations I learnt that the Italians had taken five days by sea up the coast from Shanghai to Qingdao, and that there was a further half dozen to come in a month. They had no beds or bedding, and such baggage as they possessed had been minutely examined by the Japanese and all their wine confiscated. Dr Grice had met Dr Vio, the Italian doctor, and the two of them could communicate, but the plan was that the Italians were to stay in their own little portion of the camp. They were not to communicate with the British or others, and they would be supplied with bread from the bakery, which had been a fully functioning establishment near to men's shower block No. 7 for the previous eighteen months. They would have to do their own cooking, and this caused quite a problem as they had never before cooked in 'Kongs', and they did not even know how to get a fire going. In fact, I thought that they faced a very steep learning curve if they intended to stay alive.

New Year's Day 1944 saw a concert, to which my parents went. Apparently, Fr Hanquet, a Belgian priest, paraded as Hitler, and Fr Palmers (Belgian) chased him off stage wearing a white sheepskin coat, with a sign on his back reading 'Russian Bear'. Which to the adults caused lots of laughter, but the humour and meaning just passed us boys by.

The Japanese were enforcing their policy of keeping the Italians separate from the rest of us. An Indian, Mr Ram Sabarwal, had come with them and they asked that he be removed. Mum said that Mrs Grice had told her that Mrs Sabarwal was a Japanese spy, and definitely of the faction that wanted India freed from the British Raj.

So in the middle of January, the Japanese requisitioned the men's showers and the Italian ladies were marched to the showers at 12.30 p.m. They had half an hour and were told they had to be out by 1 p.m. or the guard would extract them. Then two hours later the Italian men were marched up and given the same amount of time before being ushered back to Blocks 43 and 44. This Italian shower routine grew into a weekly affair. That 'shower day' was probably the coldest day of the year and several adults said that it looked like snow.

Dad came back from his shift to say that he had had a conversation with Dr Grice who had been called to No. 1 Kitchen because one of the cooks had been injured. Apparently Dr Vio, the Italian doctor and the only Italian who spoke English, and who had been elected their leader, had asked Dr Grice where the main camp got its supply of coal balls. He was horrified when told that each internee made some, and that they would have to do the same. He was pointedly told that if they could not bear the thought of making coal balls then they were going to be very cold.

They were also told that they had to contribute labour for the common good, including the stoking of the stove that heated the hot water tanks. But that would need discussion with the Commandant, who agreed four men was a fair number.

On 19th January, Fr Palmers, who was responsible for turning the electricity and lighting on, guessed the time wrong because his watch had stopped. This caused trouble. Fr Palmers was dragged off to solitary, denied food for 24 hours had his face repeatedly smacked, sticks put between his fingers and bent, some of his fingernails extracted. Mr McClaren made a strong protest, but it was not accepted by the Commandant as the guards had thought that the early lights had been a signal for guerrillas to break in.

Then, the next day, Mr Dhunjishah caught one of the latrine coolies stealing woollen underwear which had been hung out to dry. This misdemeanour was treated relatively lightly, because apparently the Committee considered it essential to keep up good relations with the Chinese coolies, as they provided the communications link with the outside world. The Japanese had realised that there was a need to remove human waste, and they had provided an open but waterproof cart, and four coolies pushed the empty cart into the camp. One of the Committee was always on Main Road, and as the cart passed one of the coolies spat at the Committee member, much to Japanese delight. Little did they know that out of his mouth came a tiny silk square, folded up with news, and with a message from the guerrillas surrounding the camp.

For communications to General Wang Yu Min from inside

the camp, the Committee had used balloons, into which were placed messages, detailing required supplies or discussing the practicability of a mass escape, then tied closed and put in the honey cart. Then the camp ran out of toy balloons. But apparently Mr Eggers was quite happy to donate alternatives from the medical supplies, which although white did the job, as even the scruffiest of the guards drew the line at sifting through the contents of the honey carts.

By this time the smokers were running out of supplies. For once boys were not employed to solve the problem, presumably in case we caught the habit. I saw mainly adult men, but an occasional woman, walking round the camp picking up cigarette butts. They then split them open, collected the tobacco from three or four 'dog ends', which were rolled in a small piece of paper to make a new cigarette. Thin paper became a rare commodity, and after all the 'air mail' paper had been used the desire for a smoke was so strong that people resorted to tearing pages out of Bibles. A practice I thought blasphemous ... but then I did not smoke.

Adults were still trying to organise lessons for us children, but the problem was largely the lack of paper and textbooks. Chefoo School maintained its isolationism and in fact tried to run a camp within a camp. Life is too short for petty squabbles, but the adults seemed loath to disturb the status quo. In-fighting was not confined to policy over schools. I was playing with Hazel Hoch, who was my age, and her younger brother Johnny near Block 18 when their mother came over and reported that Mr Winslow had a fight in the kitchen with Ahmed Kamal, a Turkmenistani, and that Mr Prior had tried to separate them only to have a bowl of hot curry poured over his head, and that there was now curry everywhere. Mrs Hoch then said she had fainted, and then went on to say that Miss Lindsey, a nurse, had hit Mrs Kelly with a broom and the latter had retaliated by throwing hot tea into Miss Lindsey's face. That squabble was over a bed space, so both ladies had been moved into new dormitories.

Mum sometimes went to the general swap store, called the 'Elephant Bell', which was to be found at the back of Block 24. All the children were growing and there were not enough bigger clothes to go around. Footwear presented a particular problem. The store originally started to help people who wanted to exchange sizes, but it soon developed into people charging for items, using the money to buy eggs and other necessities.

10

Another Year

Even I could understand the concern Mum had about clothes, as both Roger and I were rapidly growing out of ours. While swapping or getting given items for Roger, now a two-year-old, was relatively easy, my age made it another matter. Boys are never very caring of their clothes, and I was no different: the needle and thread was in constant use, and it became necessary to unpick knitted garments so they could be re-knitted into a larger size. I was living too rough a life for clothes to have much life in them, and previous owners had been much the same. Climbing trees, buildings, and squirreling under barbed wire fences was not the same as sitting 'quietly' on a hard school bench.

The weather started warming up in March 1944. There was a great variety of birds about, and spotting them became our main occupation for a while. The most unlikely adults turned out to be very keen ornithologists. I thought the subject very interesting, and something constructive to learn. As boys we were given a stern lecture about not climbing up to birds' nests; doctors had been selected to give the talk, and rather unexpectedly we actually heeded this advice.

There was drama at the beginning of the month when the

old bull dropped dead in the cow-shed, and that set the amateur sleuths into overdrive. Was it natural, was it poisoning or was it Anthrax? So the three cows were put into isolation, and all milk for babies stopped. Fortunately the camp had a veterinary surgeon, Doc Hoch, an American, and he was asked to perform a post-mortem. This he did and pronounced that the bull had died of natural causes, essentially old age, although I overheard mutterings among adults to the effect: 'Teach them to put young cows with an old bull.' So it was milk again for babies.

Then it was my birthday, and Mum had promised to organise a cake from the bakery, as she was no real cook herself, and I was having some friends round to tea: Peter and Michael Turner, Brian Calvert and Francis de Jong. Mum had organised some games, tame considering what we were used to getting up to, but the cake was very good.

Then Grandpa and Granny came round for supper after my party and promised some extra food, and I could hardly wait. I drowsed in my bunk reading a book that I had been given, with an ear alerted to the adults' conversation. My parents and grandparents were sitting round a table vaguely heated by the dying embers of the brick stove.

'Do you think a camp romance is likely to last?' I heard my Mum say. 'They have been thrown together here.'

Dad laughed and added, 'Don't be so pessimistic, you ought to think it romantic.'

'I'm not,' Mum said, 'Just practical. They would never have met in normal circumstances.'

Grandpa cut in, 'Who are you talking about? Have I missed some excitement or other?'

'Oh, Bert you never listen when I tell you the gossip,' my grandmother sighed. 'I told you all about that party last week on 29th February. The Spinsters' Ball the wags called it, and this engagement is the result.'

'A leap-year romance,' Dad added. From all the stokers' talk he was the better-informed one. 'She probably asked *him* to marry *her*, you can do that on a Leap Year Day.'

'You two are not funny,' Granny told them, trying to sound stern, but from my bunk it sounded more like she was about to laugh. 'I am sure that Clemmy is going to be very happy and that nice Bill Chilton is a very lucky man.'

'I wonder if she did ask him to marry her?' Mum mused; she obviously had not thought of the romance in this light before. 'But she may regret it, if she has.'

Granny, intent on getting the last word, 'I think that it's wonderful that such normal things can happen in a place like this. It shows that we are all trying to make the best of it.' The book was far more interesting so I switched off from a conversation about weddings.

On 31st March the Japanese declared that winter was over, coal issue for heating stopped and the iron pot-bellied stoves dismantled. On 3rd April Mr Eggers paid his monthly visit from the Qingdao Swiss Consulate, and in addition to a lot of medical supplies brought a small portable X-ray machine.

A week later the weather was still cold, damp and very wet. Easter Sunday fell on 9th April. All the girls had been planning to have a two-day Guide/Brownie camp in the small South Field, but this was postponed. Then Easter Monday saw the promised wedding. Now I did hear all about it, as Brian's father 'gave' the bride away. 'Clemmy' Clements, a nurse, married Bill Chilton, an accountant.

My parents both attended, so I had to be the babysitter for Roger. But I got all the details out of them. Both bride and groom had been employed by the Kailan Mining Administration. The wedding reception was in No. 2

Kitchen with tea, bread and peanut butter. Clemmy had apparently saved up for a couple of months, so a small cake was baked and decorated by Mrs Jackson from Chefoo. It was a little glimpse into normality.

Days were just passing by and our food was deteriorating in both quantity and quality. Mum and Granny spring cleaned the huts and washed winter clothes, as the temperature would hit 28°C by the end of the month. The current problem was again clothing. Children grow, and when Mum got out the clothes that I had been wearing the previous year, they were too small. Patching of clothes was ever more necessary, and we faced the issue of shoes for growing feet. Toe caps were chopped off to make room for cramped toes.

As boys we had made other plans for April. We needed reading material, as the likelihood of organised school seemed as far away as ever, after the experiments of last July at the time of the early funerals and then Fr Scanlan's gaol sentence. By pooling our observations we had worked out that one of the ground-floor rooms of the Commandant's House contained magazines. The approach was now easier as two of the dividing walls had been demolished for bricks; also the mulberry trees seemed taller and one could see the approach to the house. Thus, with a look-out up the tallest mulberry tree, I and others used to break in the window of the house, the catch being rusty, and found that we could snatch and carry away ten or so *National Geographic* magazines, and sneak them back and then divide up for reading. The plum job of this escapade was the look-out in the mulberry tree; never mind silkworms, mulberries were good to eat. The magazines were old, dated between 1890 and 1930, but the pictures were great and one could learn geography. This process carried on intermittently for the four months of summer. I cannot think that the Japanese were oblivious, but they never interfered, and the process kept us boys quiet. We ensured that only a few were in circulation, and the less damaged or used even got put back. The adults never asked, or possibly never knew, where the *National Geographic* magazines came from.

We saw a lot of new activity around the walls by workmen, supervised by the guards. When they finished one could see from the top of the hospital building that the barbed wire stretched along the top of the wall was now electrified, and there were five separate electrified barbed wire fences, including coiled barbed wire, in the 400 or so metres around the camp. Shortly after, one of the Chinese black-market tradesmen was electrocuted and his body was left on the wire for several weeks in sight of all. Then Ted McClaren reported that the Commandant said that two bags of sugar and two bottles of brandy had been found in his pockets. Ted also reported that the Commandant had complained that internees were not being respectful enough to the guards, and through that being disrespectful to the Emperor of Japan. Internees were to be instructed on the point. Ted put up a notice, which strangely enough met with the Commandant's approval.

INTERNEES WILL GIVE WAY TO UNIFORMED
MEMBERS OF HIS IMPERIAL
MAJESTY'S FORCES I.E. INTERNEES WILL
ALTER THEIR COURSE TO PORT OR
STARBOARD TO AVOID A HEAD-ON
COLLISION.

TED MCCLAREN (DISCIPLINE COMMITTEE)

Two weeks after Easter another twenty Italians arrived and

their two blocks were now getting quite full. At the end of the month the postponed Guide camp was held in the small field. The field was out of bounds for boys for four days, so we took to looking for feathered birds; I spotted a couple of Golden Orioles, and was called over to see what was supposed to be a West China Fly Catcher, dark blue bird with light grey chest, but I only just caught a glimpse. While watching, there was great excitement among the 'bird' fraternity as a 'Chestnut-bellied Rock Thrush', a bird native to India, appeared in the trees north of the hospital.

Later, on 24th May, Empire Day, there were sports on the big field. I managed to win a prize – one square of chocolate for coming first in the 440-yards in my age group.

Then great excitement came to the camp on 5th June 1944, which quite put everything else out of the minds of inmates. Rome had fallen to the Allies, and the Japanese openly allowed the information to circulate. Rumours of an invasion in France were also rife, but nobody knew anything definite. The *Peking Chronicle* grudgingly admitted the fall of Rome. Then, suddenly, the camp's morale was lifted with excitement as definite news arrived of 'D-Day' on the Normandy Beaches.

The Committee, in secret session, had decided that the interests of the camp would be better served by having 'representatives' at the Headquarters of the local guerrilla leader, General Wang. Quietly, one night, two internees, Lawrence Tipton, an Englishman who used to work in British American Tobacco, and Art Hummel, who was an American Missionary from Beijing, escaped over the wall and negotiated the barbed wire safely. Ted McClaren gave them a few hours and then reported the 'escape' to the Commandant, which safeguarded his and the Committee's position, because he knew that the Japanese would exonerate the

Committee from implication in the escape, reasoning that they would not report something they themselves planned. The escapers and other single or unaccompanied men had been housed in dormitories on the top two floors of the hospital. When their escape was discovered there was a hue and cry amongst the guard. The Head of Japanese security was replaced and within five days the younger children of the Chefoo School and their teachers were ousted from their dormitories in Blocks 23 and 24 and re-housed at the top of the hospital; the whole move to be completed in under three hours. The men who had originally been in the hospital block were temporarily housed in the Church whilst they were being interrogated. When they were released on 21st June they found that their effects had been relocated to the former Chefoo School dormitories. Whilst all this shouting was going on, I, along with most of my age group, curbed our more clandestine activities; discretion seemed the order of the day.

I asked Dad one day, 'Why have they moved everybody Dad?'

He replied 'Ronald, from the windows at the top of the hospital you could see the village to the north-east, and the Japanese suspected that candles or lights were being used to signal. By putting the younger children in those rooms they think the Chefoo teachers will control the children and that form of communication will stop.' My response was 'There are other ways of getting messages through, I believe?' Dad's silence in response to this question was confirmation enough that my discoveries were correct.

Most of the days were spent innocently playing with my soldiers. I begged a bit of the ground outside our hut from Mum, who used to grow vegetables there, mainly sweet potatoes, potatoes and tomatoes. With a frontage of two rooms it was 16 feet (5 metres) by 19 feet (6 metres) i.e. from our front wall until the next block, less the width of the path. Granny had half as much. The daily kitchen stews had a lot of cabbage, although Granny had also tried her hand with lettuce and carrots in her garden. I did not do much in the garden, preferring to augment rations by stealing maize and anything I could get my hands on from the prohibited Japanese gardens. It was not really stealing to my mind, because the Japanese employed Chinese coolies who were escorted in and out. However, some of the gardeners were sympathetic and as they only worked to midday they tended to be over-zealous in their thinning of crops, leaving them on the paths knowing that they would be clear by the next morning.

May had been a very hot month and there had been no rain. The wells were running dry: the average scoop with a bucket would now only half fill it with water. As mentioned, the wells were mostly within 16ft (5 metres) of the cesspits, and the camp doctors all felt that was too close. But the Japanese view was that they complied with their own regulations.

A couple of days later, I was innocently watching a softball match between a former Tianjin Grammar School team and Chefoo School, sitting on a low mud bank just near 3rd base. The batsman hit a possible home run, the runner on 2nd base ran past 3rd base and his knee collided with my head. I was knocked out for a moment, staggered up and ran off to my room. I was still pretty shaken so climbed into bed. An hour later Mum woke me, and as I turned over she discovered that I was bleeding from my ear. She felt that Dr Grice was needed and went and collected him from his hut. Dr Grice took one look at me and diagnosed a fracture of the skull. He then said to Mum, 'Margot, I would have liked to have

X-rayed his skull, but the machine is broken and I'm hoping that Eggers will bring the replacement parts when he comes next month. But by that time the bone will have healed. I will take him off to hospital now. He will need to be "in" for three weeks.' The camp had no stretchers, so I was carried across the camp on a door by two or three men.

Dr Grice then said I had to sleep on my back on wooden boards for the next three weeks. It did not start out very well. At first I could not sleep then, after two or three hours, sleep took over. Then the next part of the drama. Mrs Warmsley the Matron woke me up, I suppose about dawn, and shoved something into my mouth, I was used to eating and I just crunched my jaws, there was a splintering of glass. I spat it out, but Mrs Warmsley was really upset as they apparently only had a couple of thermometers. Then she realised that I had swallowed the mercury. The next thing was the bed was surrounded by virtually all the medical staff, scratching their heads. The consensus was they had no medical equipment available that would help and nature would have to be left to run its course.

The days and weeks passed by in hospital; the food was better than No. 1 Kitchen but not as good as when Mum enhanced it by adding her home-grown extra vegetables. Other than a slightly sore head, I was fit, but any attempt at sitting up, let alone at getting out of bed, brought an instant rebuke from the duty nurse or sister. I had upset Matron and that seemed to put me in purdah. But I could lift my head to peer round at my fellow patients. There were no such things as curtains to put round the beds and I was intrigued at the old man in the next bed. He had a woman doctor, Dr Gault, who used to come in twice a day with what looked about two-foot length of clear tubing and stick it down his penis and then at the other end get a small bowl of urine. The moans that the man gave out were painful to hear. To my mind it was a form of torture, and I was never voluntarily going to let anyone do that to me.

About ten days after I was admitted to hospital, Stanley Nordmo, a sixteen-year-old Chefoo schoolboy, came down from his dormitory on the upper floor. I did not know him but he introduced himself and asked after my head. He had come to apologise because it was his knee that had done the damage. I learnt that he had been blind in one eye from birth and had misjudged the distance between us. I thanked him, but in my own mind felt sorry, as he had a permanent handicap, while my sore head would be on the mend within a couple of weeks. When I was discharged, I got back to my own hut to find that I had missed a lot of rain, although I had heard it in hospital; some more mail had arrived and also the latest edition of the *Peking Chronicle*.

Towards the end of June, starting with all the medical staff, there was an outbreak of diarrhoea of epidemic proportions. At the same time, the weather broke and there was a day of heavy rain, a real downpour. So many were sick that roll call took a couple of hours. The next day the Japanese medical team arrived. The Japanese were paranoid about a cholera outbreak. So we were all lined up outside the hospital, everybody had a glass rod shoved up their behind; then after a test of the surface the glass rod it was wiped in alcohol and then shoved up the next candidate. There were at least five teams and the whole process took all day, although as originally planned the men were to be first, then the women and then those under fifteen. But the children under seven started bawling for their Mums and chaos reigned. One certain thing you could say is that it was unpleasant while it lasted, and I got rather tired of looking at bare behinds. But probably not as unpleasant as when we got inoculations for whatever was the current threat of disease. As an example, shortly after the cholera scare, there was a big line-up for a typhoid inoculation, but one had to gauge one's place in the queue carefully, as needles were in short supply. The needle was changed about every 100 inoculations.

Then came 4th July, which was American Independence Day. I could not see why we were celebrating American independence – after all they had rejected the British Crown – but I suppose that it pleased someone. Sports were held in the afternoon and I did not do so well this time. America challenged England to a game of softball. The game went well and the result was England 30 USA 6. The band burst into 'God Save the King' and the guards, who had mostly been stationed pre-war in embassies throughout the world, all stood with us to attention and saluted. (Pavlovian reflex?) Anyhow, it was obvious the Commandant was not amused. That evening a supper dance was held for those over fifteen and I got saddled with being a babysitter for Roger again.

A week later fifteen more Italians and Mrs Bryson arrived from Beijing. They brought very cheery news about the overall war situation. The *Peking Chronicle* also reported the assassination attempt on Hitler.

The weather turned once again to rain and thunderstorms. This played havoc with my scrounging, because I left distinctive foot-prints everywhere: I had acquired a pair of football boots with a tread of two bars and two studs, and now everybody would know where I had been.

The warmth brought the scorpions out from the remaining walls, the presence of which had been used as an excuse for the Japanese to demolish some of the walls, when the real reason was that the camp wanted use of the bricks. The current craze was scorpion fights; they would not cross a ring of ash, so us boys we selected a scorpion, and the dangers

My parents' wedding.

RB in front of cousins
at Peitaho.

Top: Tianjin Club skating rink, 1938
Above: Flooding in Tianjin, 1939.

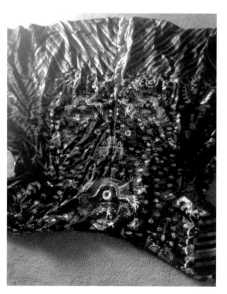

Mandarin coat. Rank: Blue Bird.

Weihsien Camp

Guard in pillbox.

Inmates' huts.

Top left:
Weihsien
pillbox.

Top right:
No. 2
Kitchen.

Weihsien Church

Accommodation huts.

Weihsien, Japanese HQ.

Water queue 1944.

Internal gate.

Weihsien hospital water tower

Weihsien inmates on eve of release, 17th August 1945, taken by the main gate.

US Sergeant,
communications
expert.

Weihsien, aerial view.

RB and Roger in Peking.

Peking, Summer Palace.

made the whole process more exciting. We used to pick the creatures by going in over their heads, where the sting in the tail did not reach. There was a skill in this, and whilst I never got stung others did. We kept our scorpions in reclaimed jars, holes punched in screw top. The procedure was that two picked out their scorpions and placed them in the ring, the scorpions then attacked each other and when one was dead the owner of the other got points. Mum never found out about scorpion fights because she would have created a dreadful fuss.

At the end of the day of scorpion-fighting the winning owner, if lucky, got a boiled sweet. The sad part of this game was that none of the scorpions lasted very long. A champion rarely survived more than three or four fights. It was a pity but we felt that we were doing the camp inmates a favour by ridding the area of scorpions.

I was rarely in our two rooms in Block 13 during the day. After breakfast and roll call, I was off somewhere in the camp running wild without supervision. Meals, however, were too important to miss and my friends, like me, ate in their own huts, so we all went back for lunch, our main meal and supper, usually some kind of soup and bread. I was not allowed out after supper except on the light summer evenings when there were semi-organised games on the sports field; otherwise I was taught various games of cards.

Dad was still a stoker at No. 1 Kitchen. He would come back from the evening shift very dirty and tired. He was a tall man, six foot three, with a moustache and nearly bald head. Thirty-eight when he first entered camp, he had then weighed just over 90 kgs; he ended up at 50 kgs. The lack of soap made it hard for him to get clean and I think this was the thing he found most difficult. Cold showers were all right in the summer but it was almost impossible to get rid of greasy black coal dust, especially without much soap. Roger took a lot. I, personally, never worried and in the winter, since I only liked hot or at least warm water, I hardly ever washed: the legs below my shorts were always grey with dirt, ground into the chapped skin. My father did get me into the men's showers at least once a week, but without adequate soap this made little impression on long-term dirt. All my friends were in just the same state.

Then came a major local drama. The Commandant had received orders to seize all passports, against a receipt from him. Half the camp refused, and thus the decree became: no passports, no receipts and thus no food. The Japanese got their way. Surprisingly the passports were still there in the Commandant's Office when the camp was liberated. I think the Kempetai had concluded that if you did not have a passport you could not escape, because you had no identity!

The usual 9 a.m. roll call had been augmented by another at 7 p.m., the logic of which I could not understand. When Tipton and Hummel had made their escape, their subsequent absence had been obvious during morning roll call, and anybody else escaping would surely follow their lead and do so at night, not during the day: so the morning roll call should have been enough. Somehow, the evening roll calls always took longer. On 16th August, at the 7 p.m. roll call, boredom had again set in: not only did the number within each group have to tally, but then the guards had to add up the totals. Any doubt and the whole camp had to be re-counted. The electric wiring in the camp was looped about anything and ran at varying heights. It was particularly low in front of the hospital (Block 61). To relieve the boredom of waiting during roll call, the Chefoo School students, mainly the twelve- to sixteen-year-olds, used to jump up and touch the wires.

One day the current was obviously 'on', as someone got himself burnt, but another, Brian Thompson, being very tall, had reached up and just gripped the wire – he was instantly electrocuted. Dr Grice was called and then Dr Robinson (Kailan Mining) and Dr Howie (Chefoo), because they were further away; the three carried out artificial respiration for nearly three hours, but to no avail.

Brian's funeral was the next day, but Brian's parents, who were in the camp, ruled that it would be private, for Chefoo only, the first and only restriction placed on attendance at a funeral, but then the parents were missionaries.

The next week heavy rain fell each day. But then on 21st August 1944 Mr Eggers made an unscheduled visit, escorting 400 American Red Cross parcels. A big parcel contained four parcels each about 12 inches (30cm) square and 6 inches (15cm) deep.[59] Eggers said they were for all the camp but had no detailed instructions. The American Missionaries claimed that they were American Red Cross parcels for Americans, and that the British could make their own arrangements and obviously had not. Not that any American in the camp had had anything to do with the organisation of the parcels. Many of the individual Americans shared out some of the contents with their non-American friends, as they could not accept the policy of their camp leaders.

September was almost a non-month: it rained constantly, everything got and remained damp, and the air was sticky, although in the last week one Canadian and three American nuns were shipped to Beijing; the story had it that they needed operations. Those of us in the junior 'mafia' thought that some of the unaccompanied men staying at Weihsien might have been involved, and as a result the resident Bishop thought a change of venue for his charges was indicated.

On 1st October, the guards moved the evening roll call,

which was brought forward to start at 6.30 p.m. Then a new timetable was issued: 8.15 a.m. Breakfast; 9 a.m. Roll call; 1.15 p.m. Tiffin;[60] 5.45 p.m. Supper.[61]

Two weeks later coal was issued to allow fires to be lit; there was a great rush to make and dry coal balls. Using the scoop that Grandpa had made me, I managed to keep the worst of the coal dust at bay. After September being so wet, the weather was dry but the temperature dropped to 5°C. Rumours abounded, not helped by different interpretations of the *Peking Chronicle*, which although in English was edited by Germans.

One day in mid-October, I came across Suzanne Twyford-Thomas on Main Street, full of the news that her father, who was a cook, had met with rather a nasty accident in his kitchen. He'd been trying to push the small amount of meat available through the mincer when part of his finger went through the machine. With great presence of mind Mr Twyford-Thomas, with someone holding a piece of paper with his finger on it, walked from No. 2 Kitchen to the hospital, where Dr Grice sewed it back on. I thought it interesting, but it did not affect me as Mum got our stews from No. 1 Kitchen.

Towards the end of the month the Japanese did a surprise search for stove pipes, because they considered that there were too many stoves. With perfect Tokyo logic the search started at Block 1. Quick calculation suggested that we would be the 100th room to be searched. Fortunately, I was out in the 'garden' re-fighting the battle of the Somme with toy soldiers, complete with trenches. It was a very quick case of soldiers back in box, stove pipes buried in the trench and covered with mud and all smoothed over; meanwhile Mum had covered the brick stove with a pile of clothes and was now gardening! Had the oven been lit at the time, it would have been a different story. We would have contributed to the contents of the truck that was being rapidly filled with a huge assortment of tins. With only one iron stove in sight, Mum was praised for our frugality. Mum told Dad what had happened when he got back from his stoker shift, so plans were made to substitute a quickly removable stove pipe.

The month ended with a great rat hunt, as with colder weather they were coming in. The walls were a perfect place for them to hide, as the bricks were all laid on their edges, with longitudinal ones spanning the width of the wall and a flat brick face on the front and back. A perfect haunt for scorpions in the summer and rats in the winter. The nearest I'd come to the latter was hearing them scrabbling round near to my head when lying in my bunk.

Elsewhere, the coal issue was stoking passions. It was in short supply and people were trying to measure coal dust using an egg-cup, which usually ended up in blows being exchanged. Suddenly the supply of flour plummeted, and bread became severely rationed. Kitchens even ran out of kaoliang (millet), while I had not seen any meat for weeks.

I then thought that I should try and exploit my hole into the Japanese compound. Discovering that it was very close to the coal supply to two of the guards' houses, and reasoning that a few lumps of coal would go unnoticed, I took the opportunity of tucking a couple of lumps under my coat to take home. It was such a change from coal balls to burn. Meanwhile I started 'acquiring' wood from the coal yard; there was a lot of good firewood but I had to take bricks out of a wall to climb over, throw the wood over the wall and then climb back. Then carry the wood back to our hut and start making coal balls. A week after the scheme started the Japanese decided to build a tennis court in the coal yard, so it was back to the drawing-board to keep warm.

Mum was visited by Mrs Grice and Granny Fleet came in, and the usual exchange of news and gossip took place. I overheard that when Mrs Vio (Italian doctor's wife) arrived in Weihsien she met the Commandant and, not knowing who he was, said 'Very nice place, lots of trees.' The Commandant was pleased, but changed his mind when she added, 'In Shanghai we heard lots about the black market and the shopping going on: where is the street with all the little shops and market stalls?' Much adult laughter. Rumours in Weihsien were rife, but they always had some grains of truth – the key was to sort the chaff from the dust.

Up until this point in time, all the camp guards had originally been members of Japan's Consular Police, selected for service in foreign countries; they wore quite distinctive black uniforms. Slowly these disappeared, obviously needed for army service. They were replaced by army soldiers clad in khaki, and it was noticeable that the guards' age dropped dramatically: many of the new cohort were probably only three or four years older than I, and most of them were almost shorter than their rifles. Overhearing bits of adult conversation, and using my imagination, I put two and two together: it seemed that the 'adult' Japanese Army was being replaced by schoolboys, and it was natural for these 'new' soldiers to be a little more vicious than their predecessors. The local Commandant got what the army gave him, all now draftees, and they lacked the training and discipline of the regular Consular Police. In many cases the draftees were teenagers from the streets of Tokyo or Nagasaki; looking back, if in Britain the British Army recruited teenagers from Birmingham, the Gorbals or South Yorkshire, gave them a rifle for authority and very little training, they would probably have acted the same. Incidents of face-slapping increased. Almost daily there was proof that this was the fundamental measure of discipline within the Japanese Army: the Generals slapped the Colonels, who slapped the Majors, who slapped the Captains … so by the time you reached the 2nd Class impressed Private, he had only got Koreans or internees to slap. The Commandant was equivalent to a Captain, but when an external inspection occurred the higher ranks were evident.

In 1944 there was a very poor harvest in north-east China and this was reflected in the food, which declined both in quantity and quality. There had been days when no flour was delivered, others when the flour was little more than a heaving mass of weevils. We got millet instead, which is a small-grained, annual warm-weather cereal belonging to the grass family, and usually sold as birdseed in Europe and America. Millet is highly tolerant to extreme weather conditions such as drought and is nutritious compared to the major cereals, such as rice and wheat. The personal vegetable gardens by the inmates worked, as non-interned friends fortunately kept up the supply of seeds as these could be put in envelopes with letters and did not have the high 'loss' rate of parcels.

The Swiss representatives Mr Joerg and Mr Eggers went round the camp, and spoke to the vegetable workers in the hospital kitchen. They walked into the Sewing Room to find a Japanese guard behind the door with his trousers off, getting them sewn. Then one of the camp inmates came in to have his shorts repaired. Miss Clements, who had been a nurse at the Kailan Mines hospital, shouted out: 'Do not take your shorts off, there is one man behind the door already with his off!'

After a very cold wet October it turned quite warm and sunny. I went back with others to the acquisition of *National Geographics* and soon the last of them had been nicked, read and some returned. One day a bit of a tragedy struck: a warning came from Peter, the look-out in the mulberry tree, that guards were approaching. So we scarpered. I was the last out and a rifle-swinging guard caught my left knee with his rifle butt. I carried on running and got well out of the prohibited zone, and reached home despite being barely able to walk. The knee ached for days, but I dared not admit that I had been up to no good, definitely in Japanese eyes, probably in my parents', but certainly there would be trouble from some quarter.

There was a big show-down outside Block 24, which now held adult women. On a cold wet morning, having been counted at roll call, the women immediately went back inside. King Kong[62] saw them and ordered them to stand for half an hour in the wet. They retaliated by dancing and skipping. King Kong went apoplectic, jumped on to a little platform and addressed them in Chinese, saying that he had been greatly insulted; if we had been in India the authorities would have hung them up by their thumbs.

He knew that they called him names, but they were lucky that he did not take one of them and shoot them as an example for causing a Japanese to lose face. King Kong then went into Mrs Buist's block which was across the Rocky Road from ours, and ordered her to stand on parade for roll call. Mrs Buist, a Salvation Army officer, refused to leave her three children, the eldest of whom was six. King Kong called her an 'addled egg' in Chinese.

Next day King Kong took roll call again and ended with 'OK, ladies thank you.' He had decided to be polite and ignore insults. The previous day he had arrived at the roll call saying 'I'll dig the old sows out of their beds if they are not already standing to be counted.'

However, in early December, a Japanese guard went up

to Mrs Howard-Smith, a nurse, and slapped her face when she was not lining up to his satisfaction outside the hospital. Ted McClaren reported it to the Commandant. King Kong was livid and upset, and said that if he was reported again he, King Kong, would have to commit hari-kari[63] and it would be on McClaren's conscience.

The next day King Kong brought a dozen bottles of beer to men working in the bakery. They reported that he was staggering, but they accepted the beer. On the way back to the guard room we watched him pull out his sword and have a fight with a tree. A few days later one of the guards got very drunk, went into Block 24, sat on a box and said he felt sick. One of the ladies got him a bowl, he heaved violently, lay down on Miss Dorea Harper's bed and went to sleep. He had to be removed by Ted McClaren, helped by another Japanese guard.

A few days later I was messing around with Peter and Brian and we heard aircraft very high, I could see them clearly. Then one came a lot lower and I could see the twin fuselages and I found out later that they were P38 Lockheed Lightnings. King Kong came out of the guardroom and fired his Mauser at the aircraft, I suppose it made him feel good, but the chances of hitting an aircraft were nil. The three of us were very impressed by the aeroplanes, and decided that aviation was where one's career would head, instead of into a dull old office.[64]

**

Shandong Province, being on the coast, fell within that part of China conquered by Japan in 1937, hence there was in place a sort of civil government, with a Japanese bias. The Japanese Foreign Office was involved with the running of the camps, and after the 1942 diplomatic exchange of personnel, they put in place a guard force over which they had control. These were the personnel who formed our first guards. Most of them had at least a smattering of English. Whilst they were very jealous of their standing amongst enemy nationals, and hated to 'lose face', they were not gratuitously cruel. I experienced a marked change from the army personnel in Tianjin. Weihsien was probably the only POW/Internee camp to have this experience. Further south in China it was a battle zone, with open warfare raging south and west of Shanghai. The Japanese Army controlled the camps, except that in a lot of cases the Commandant had been in the Consular service. This could have been because he would have spoken at least a little English. Hong Kong, Singapore, Philippines, Borneo and the Netherlands East Indies were conquered territories, since 8th December 1941, and under the complete control of the Japanese military, mostly army, but there were some navy camps in the Celebes and Japan. The Japanese ethos was you should never surrender but rather fall on your sword. Thus captured Allied military were held beneath contempt, whereas Allied civilians fell between Japan's two schools of thought. The civilians represented a hated regime, but women and children, for one, were not expected to have graduated to the hari-kari tradition – they were considered too stupid.

It was very educational being in one of our rooms when Mrs Grice and her friends came to visit Mum. I got early word that Susie Grice was taking part in a pantomime, being put on for Christmas. Susie, with the passing of two years, had moved on from being a tomboy with me and my friends to be a proper teenager.

Apparently Drs Grice and Robinson had had a complaint from the Rev Longman that the women's ward in the hospital was like bedlam, or a church meeting. There were loud guffaws and he had seen one visitor jump into a patient's bed when he was visiting his wife. Dr Grice had even written a letter to Rev Longman for details. Ted McClaren was asked to mediate but Longman said: 'Forget it, just hush it up!'

Christmas Day 1944 came and went; most people had been allowed to order from Grefen and Wildes, a German-run grocery shop in Qingdao. They had shortages too and everybody had been rationed to one tin of jam, and there was no lard, bacon, butter or fat. On Boxing Day, the temperature didn't rise above -12°C, too cold to make coal balls. Fortunately, I had made as many as I could when the temperature had been warmer, so we didn't suffer too much.

11

Is this the Last Year?

The Camp Liaison Committee expressed to the Commandant that there was no soap – I had known this for over a year. Also, with winter weather come, there was neither enough coal nor flour. That parcels had stopped arriving, and when they did they were damaged. By 8th January the coal ration was cut off for three days each week, which meant four scuttlefuls each week per household. I tried to help by mixing a little more mud in with coal balls, but found that, in using a 50/50 formula, they failed to burn. Mum was furious that I had changed the recipe and hence wasted coal. But I had reckoned that the raw coal was variable in quality anyway, often with a lot of crushed stone mixed in, and actually the failed coal balls were easy to cure. Break up the adulterated coal balls – they were only sun-dried – mix in a bit of water, add an extra dose of coal dust and remake the coal balls with beefed-up coal content. This proved successful.

Dad came back and said that the Committee had been in to see the Commandant again, who accepted the situation but said that they could not get food, and that parcels could not come from Tianjin as the railway was constantly under attack from bandits.

There had been half a dozen deaths since the New Year. There was a 'flu' epidemic, Mum said. We got small bits of horse meat for tiffin as a change, and it was actually very tasty. Also a supply of flour, enough for eight days. Only twenty-one copies of the *Peking Chronicle* arrived. The weather was still bitterly cold, plummeting to -12°C every day.

On 25th January another 400 big American Red Cross parcels arrived. Captain Tsukiyama said they were to be divided, one small parcel per person. Which meant, I thought, that the Bridge family would get one big parcel containing four small parcels. Terrible rows began from the Americans, whose stance again was: 'They are US Red Cross parcels paid for by US taxes hence not to be given to foreigners.' I overheard Dad saying that the ringleaders of the American rebellion were both tobacco experts who had lived in China for a number of years with their Russian wives. He doubted if they had ever been in America for long enough to pay a penny in tax there. Captain Tsukiyama said he would go to Qingdao and clarify the distribution of parcels; meanwhile, parcel distribution was on hold. The atmosphere in the camp grew poisonous; people vented their anger by resorting to fists and flinging mud at the Americans. I kept a low profile while these exchanges were going on because I could see no advantage in getting involved.

Four days later Captain Tsukiyama returned from Qingdao to say that instructions from Tokyo were that a small parcel was to be issued to each inmate, and the medical supplies were for the hospital. Then Dad came back into the room and said that Captain Tsukiyama added that, if inmates did not agree with the Tokyo directive, there would be no parcels for Weihsien and they would be sent back to Tokyo. The Americans reluctantly accepted the directive over the parcels, but still maintained that it was unlawful for US goods to be given to other nationals. The Committee confirmed the ruling: one small parcel per head.

The Red Cross parcels were distributed, despite continuing American objections. The medical supplies consisted of a lot of boxes and we all helped carrying them to the hospital. There were lots of books too, but these all had to go to the Commandant's House to be vetted. Even newspapers arrived, saying that the end of war in Europe was coming soon, on 4th February. Mum and Dad did not believe this since there would have been some reaction from the Commandant if it were even half true. Then they went back to what they intended doing that day. Tobacco leaves were removed from their hiding place behind the kaoliang stalks of the ceiling, Mum stripped the stalks off and Dad pounded the rest of the leaves to near dust before rolling a few cigarettes.

Another distribution of Red Cross goods, razors and blades, some soap, toothbrushes and toothpaste. Mum now allowed us butter and jam for tea. Sometimes, we even got some Spam[65] out of a tin from the parcels. Mrs Grice came round for sympathy, as when the 'end of war' rumours had surfaced she had been very vocal about how it would serve Hitler right. Mrs Gerber, the German wife of an American, had complained to Ted McClaren about her remarks. Then, when that complaint had received an unsympathetic response, Mrs Gerber went round to Mrs Grice's hut and tried to start a fight.

Mum got a food parcel from Freda; miraculously untouched by postal or customs authorities, so the contents were intact. Previous parcels from her had up to half the contents rifled.

Then bartering started about a week after the distribution of the Red Cross parcels, the 'exchange rate' generally on a standard scale. A pound-tin of milk powder went for three small tins of jam, or four tins of Spam. No equivalent price was quoted for a small packet of ten cigarettes.

There was much drama in the Italian part of the camp, where two ladies went berserk. One, the Korean wife of an Italian, stripped herself naked and was found in Fr Rutherford's room; the other kept rushing round camp clad in only the thinnest of nightdresses. In the end she was apprehended and put in a locked room on her own.

I got given a pair of shoes that Dad managed to sew up; I had spent most of that winter in an old pair of football boots, but the stitching fastening the soles to the uppers had eventually worn through. I was playing outside the de Jongs' rooms in Block 22, kicking a ball around with Eric Liddell, the former Olympic gold medallist who was teaching us the finer points of soccer. I knew Mr Liddell quite well, not only from camp life, but also because he was a great friend of Dad's, as they used to run against each other in the 1920s and play rugger together in the 1930s. In fact Eric's parents had known Dad's parents. Eric Liddell suddenly collapsed, unconscious, and as some rushed off to find a doctor, I went across to Block 23, as I knew that there was a stack of doors in the basement, and a couple of us grabbed one and by the time we got back most of the doctors in the camp were there. Eric Liddell was put on the door and carried to the hospital. I went back to our block and told Mum and Dad what had happened. The incident occurred mid-afternoon, and by the evening we heard that he had died of a brain tumour and haemorrhage.

Real drama occurred on 3rd March 1945. My birthday had passed off as a really tame affair and I was trying to go to sleep when a lot of pistol firing was heard coming from the sports field. I looked out to see what was happening, and saw two guards dressed in white ju-jitsu[66] clothes tearing down Rocky Road towards the Japanese quarters. I was woken up just after midnight by more shouting and lots of shots. I wanted to go and see what was happening but was told to stay in bed.

Next morning I went to look for someone who could tell me what all the firing in the night had been about. I met up with Brian whose hut was across Main Street from the Guard House. Apparently the guards had been having a ju-jitsu competition outside the Guard House and one of the contestants accused another of cheating. One then chased another to the sports field where the firing of Mausers started up. Then the two, thought to be Bushinde[67] and King Kong, disappeared to the Japanese Club for more beer. They came across another guard, whose nickname was Soapy Sam, and chased him in their ju-jitsu pyjamas back to the Guard House. Meanwhile the rest of the guards were having a riot in the sports field, shooting in the air to try and quieten things down. Soapy Sam then ran back to near Block 50 to try and hide. King Kong, despite being a Sergeant, emerged but events proved he had no control. Suddenly, with no more beer to drink, the guards went off and the incident fizzled out.

After discussing the drama of the night before, Brian and I then went off to see if we could find any ammunition. There were lots of empty cartridge cases lying about. Then in the far corner I could see my young brother Roger holding a Mauser machine pistol, pointing at another four-year-old boy, trying to pull the trigger, saying 'Bang, bang, you're dead'. The trigger was fortunately too stiff for his little fingers. I was able to disarm him and gave the gun to Ted McClaren, who had arrived by then. He unclipped the magazine and took the gun to the Commandant. Where the Mauser's wooden holster was I had no idea: they usually came with a big wooden holster that doubled as a butt, converting the weapon to a shoulder gun, and one usually saw it with its leather carrying straps.

There were few guards in evidence for the next few days. The camp rumour was that Voshida, King Kong, Soapy Sam and Bushinde had all gone to Qingdao for an investigation. What was fact was that two Kempetai officers now strutted round the camp, and Eggers arrived but was surrounded by guards and no one could get nearer than five yards to him.

Then more US aircraft flew over, very high, and through my mind again went the thought: 'That's the life for me.'

Watanabe, a guard also known as Golliwog, started an official rats and mice extermination scheme. Then another 150 US Red Cross big parcels arrived, but were turned round and sent to Beijing immediately, presumably for the priests and nuns. The delegation of guards returned from Qingdao and there was another big party in their Club which spilt out down Cow Lane, at the south end of Main Street.

On 11th March 1945 Dad had banked up the stove for the night, and he opened the door to let the smoke out. One of the six Alsatians used by the Japanese as 'fierce' police dogs wandered in wagging its tail, and came up to me. I tried to give him a piece of crust but he would not eat it. Mum said: 'The dog is probably foreign-owned, it is not very fierce, and I'm sure that you, Ronald, have seen them playing with the five- and six-year-old children.'

'Mum, I have seen that and the dogs are always very friendly to me. But, some of the boys I go round with are frightened and any dog senses the fear and growls. Then the children panic.'

The next morning I had some real oatmeal porridge for breakfast, which was such a welcome change from millet. Then back to the daily chore of making coal balls. I had acquired a length of open tin drainpipe which I rigged behind the brick stove, and there I finished off drying the coal balls while the fire was on, as it seemed to make them burn better when they were used the next day.

In mid-April Mum was suddenly fussing round to find a suitable dress whilst Dad was protesting that he had lost so much weight that his suit would never fit him. The occasion was the christening of the little Chilton baby girl, born in early March. I was out of the equation.

Mrs Grice came round and said that Dr Grice had had to X-ray King Kong, the guard Sergeant, as he'd injured his foot playing tennis. The X-ray machine had evidently been repaired. But King Kong had let out that the wall shutting off the Italians would soon be removed and that there was going to be freedom of movement within the camp. With the change of weather in April there came a plague of flies. The culprits we could smell: a faint sickly stench from the thawing of the rats' bodies in our walls. Suddenly those of us who did not have a school to go to were mobilised. There were no fly swats, so we were encouraged to swat the flies with a bare hand, which was none too clean as coal balls were still being made. As an inducement the adults introduced a policy that increased the death rate of flies enormously. When a boy or girl filled a large match-box (about the size of an old Swan Vesta box) with 'bodies' and then presented it to the adult supervisor it was exchanged for one square of chocolate from a Hershey chocolate bar[68] out of the food parcels. Then empty the box, which was checked as truly 'empty'. Then one could start after more flies. On a good day one could manage two boxes. I, like others, then used the same hands, covered in their congealed coal dust and squashed fly dirt, to put the chocolate in my mouth to savour. This purge got the flies out of the camp, yet surprisingly none of the 'fly squad' reported any gastric trouble. In fact, from my subsequent experience, this addition of 'fly dirt' to my diet has ensured that I have had a 'cast-iron' stomach for more than seventy years!

Saturday 14th April the wall around the Italian Quarter came down. There was no general mingling of the Italians and the original inhabitants of Weihsien, though individual cases of friendliness did occur between the prisoners.

On May 3rd Mr Sabarwal, an 'Indian' whose British passport had expired in 1923, and who had long been suspected of being a Japanese stool pigeon, announced to the Committee that Germany had surrendered, but the camp was not to be told. Dad came in with the news half an hour after the Committee meeting. It was being openly talked about by the evening.

Two days later the *Peking Chronicle* arrived with the same news. At 11 p.m. that night two teenagers climbed the bell tower of Block 23 and started tolling the bell, which served as the Fire Alarm. Sgt Bushinde got very drunk, whilst all the rest of the guards were rushing round like headless chickens. Then one of them started the siren at the gate, but no one knew what that meant, least of all the guards. King Kong decided that at 1 a.m. there was to be a roll call and told Ted McClaren, who had to agree. Then Sergeant Bushinde ruled that guards would drag inmates from their beds if necessary. With twenty minutes' notice we spent an hour in the dark and cold. When it was over Mum announced that, as we had a little millet bread back at the hut, she was going to open a tin of salmon for a late-night feast. The consensus of opinion, amongst the adults, was that it had all been a stupid incident, but I never did find out what Mr Cotterill and the former Miss Hills, both Assembly of God missionaries, thought of it all: they had been married less than twelve hours when kicked out of bed for a roll call.

Thanksgiving services were held to mark the end of the war in Europe by all religions at their regular services in the Church on the following Sunday, May 6th. The rest of the month was quite calm, except the guards got drunk with beer at their Club each evening; fortunately they could not make it to the internees' camp, but one could hear them bumbling about in their area. Which was to us of course 'out of bounds'.

Over a month later I overheard Mrs Grice, who had called round for 'coffee', talking to Mum. Mrs Grice admitted that she found it impossible to get their daughter Susie to do housework, that she had asked her husband to speak to Susie, which he had done, but the result was nil. She did apparently let Susie sleep outside; but Mum would not let me, and I felt deeply jealous. Apparently the night before a guard had come round, roared like a lion and ordered Susie 'in', as all the camp had to sleep inside. The mothers decided to have a meeting because the mosquitoes and sand flies were an irritant, as were bed bugs, which with the warmer weather emerged from the wood in the beds, or the kaoliang of the ceiling insulation.

So I got sent round to gather all the Tianjin mothers to one of our rooms, Block 13 Room 11, on 18th June. A whole host arrived and I tried to hide as a fly on the wall, but was told I could not stay for the meeting, but I definitely remained within earshot. Mrs Grice said Susie had been ordered quite politely by the guard.

Then Mrs Marshall said that she had insisted that her two sons, aged seven and four, could not sleep in their hut because of the bed bugs. Sergeant Bushinde said it was easy to get rid of bed bugs. You needed three long pieces of wood then with a big needle put lots of small holes in them and place them the length of the bed under the mattress. Then go to sleep. The bugs come out and bite you then run to sleep it off in the holes. In the morning get hold of the wood, remove it from the bed and quietly pour boiling water and they die. To which Mrs Marshall, who spoke Japanese, said 'I suppose you write on the wood: all bugs sleep here.'

Bushinde replied 'It is not necessary.' Complete collapse of assembled ladies when Mrs Marshall translated what had been said. The ladies decided that they would petition the Committee to get Japanese approval for all under fourteen to sleep outside, weather permitting.

Dad had been co-opted to serve on the Camp Administrative Committee due to the long-term sickness of the original Kitchen No. 1 representative. Thus Mum got all the scuttlebutt accurately reported, and I was a very eager listener to their exchanges.

As June 1945 dawned, my friends and I remained totally without discipline, as the heat and lack of food rendered the adults lethargic. Those blackboards once destined for the school, and which hadn't proved of much use, as there was no chalk, had all ended up burnt as firewood. So no chance of lessons. Paper and pencils were unobtainable. The Chefoo School, though, functioned as normal, and still considered themselves above us 'town urchins'; they maintained their self-proclaimed status as superior 'public schoolboys'. To prove *our* superiority in all things mischievous, several of us conceived a cunning plan. There were several cesspits in camp, which were emptied by Chinese coolies allowed in for the purpose. One of the American children, one Art Kelly, had fallen into a cesspit early on. Fortunately his sister had seen the accident and had called their mother, who got him out, but he stank for days and had to live with the name 'Smelly Kelly' for the rest of the war. After this, wooden covers were made and fitted over all the cesspits. But the incident had given us an idea.

One cesspit, near the hospital, was not far from one of the paths that went round inside the walls of the camp, along which the Japanese guards patrolled at night. The path was defined by white-painted stones so the guard could see the way. In the twilight one evening, several of us got together and moved the white stones, diverting the path from its original trajectory, which bypassed the cesspit, so now it defined a gentle curve straight towards it. We removed the covering boards too. We imagined the guard's face when he stumbled and fell, and thought the incident would be very funny. It was only a pity that we would be back in our huts with our parents if the plan came to fruition, but nevertheless it had been fun to do, and not that easy to move the stones without being seen. I went back to our hut and had supper of soup and a crust. Then I went to bed and forgot all about the cesspit and the path, as I think most of us did.

Next morning I woke to the sound of Dad shouting in annoyance. Apparently he had gone across to collect breakfast to find the Kitchen in uproar. I was surprised, for he seldom got really cross, but I was not long kept in the dark.

'Ronald, did you or your friends have anything to do with moving the stones on the path by the hospital?' he demanded at once.

I was not quite sure how to reply, so stayed quiet.

'Were you involved?' he said again, suspiciously.

'What stones?' Mum put in, giving me a chance to stay silent.

'Those white stones that outline the path for people to see at night,' Dad explained.

'Well what happened?' Mum inquired as she dished out our millet porridge, but for once I had lost my appetite.

'Those white stones were moved so that the path, instead of running past the cesspit went straight into it,' Dad told her, 'and the boards were removed as well.'

'Does it matter that much?' she asked.

'One of the new young guards was nearly killed last night when he fell in.'

Foolishly, I blurted out 'Did a guard fall in then?'

'He did and he would have drowned if his rifle hadn't stuck across the pit and given him something to hang on to.'

Mum giggled and I did too. 'You mean one of the guards fell in and had to stay there hanging on to his rifle,' she laughed. 'Serves him right.'

'Not really. The poor fellow was stuck for two hours until the next guard patrol found him up to his shoulders in the cesspit contents, so I believe he is very lucky to be still alive.'

'He must smell awful.' I breathed happily. Our plan had succeeded. A perfect conclusion.

'Maybe he does, but his superiors are not amused and have reported the incident to Ted McClaren to carry out a full investigation. The Discipline Committee intends to do something about it.'

I now saw why Dad was so cross and my heart dropped. There was going to be real trouble.

'So will you please tell me, Ronald, did you have anything to do with the incident? Did you move the stones or help at all with this prank?'

I could hardly say no and lie to my father, but I was afraid to say yes so I stayed silent and wished that I had got up earlier and disappeared before the storm broke.

'Answer me,' Dad persisted. From his expression I knew it was no use. I would have to say something and the only thing I could say was the truth.

'There are lots of gangs of kids round camp,' Mum put in. 'It doesn't have to be Ronald's crowd.'

'It doesn't have to be, it won't be the Chefoo School lot – they are too pie, I have a feeling our son was involved.'

There was nothing for it but to admit what I had done, although I refused to tell who had been with me. Keeping silent was of little use anyway, because our parents knew who was in the various 'gangs', as did the other parents.

The Discipline Committee decided that we should all be walloped, which was duly administered. The 'trial' and punishment was reported to the Commandant who accepted it and the matter was considered closed. We then discovered why the Japanese had not made a big issue of the incident: the guard had been drunk when he fell in the cesspit, so we had got away lightly.

We all gathered together away from our huts later on when we had taken our punishment and gloated over our success. We had found that there were plenty of adults who thought the incident very amusing, as indeed had Mum. It would have all been very different had the guard drowned. In conceiving the plan we had thought that at best we would trip someone or they would get a shoe full of sewage. We had to suffer some punishment to mollify the Commandant. But our street credence soared, and all the adults suddenly acknowledged us. The Chefoo schoolteachers warned their pupils that we were agents of the devil and must be ignored. Encounters were definitely to be restricted to games on the sports field, and then, without exception, under supervision.

Towards the end of June 1945 Dad came in to say that the Commandant, Captain Tsukiyama, and his Deputy, Lieutenant Voshida, were both to be transferred to Nanking. July saw Mr Eggers and Mr Engstrom (another Swiss Consul) arrive with lots of tins and medical supplies, and with the news that Mr Joerg would be coming the following day.

Tsukiyama and his team had been to the last Committee meeting to explain the move. Mr Izu was to be the new Commandant, with Sergeant King Kong promoted to Lieutenant, and he would also hold the position of Deputy Commandant; this was cancelled three weeks later, and Koyanagi became head of the Consular Police, who were the official guards. Mr Joerg duly arrived and was welcomed by the Japanese and went to the hospital to meet the staff and patients.

The transfer of these guards meant their replacements were either retired soldiers or teenagers. Grandpa took a gloomy view of it all. He voiced the opinion, 'that with pensioners and boys replacing the regular guard, it is the beginning of the end.'

Granny replied 'Well that is what we want. The war in Europe has ended, surely it will end here.'

'They are removing the able-bodied men and replacing them with crocks and babes,' Grandpa said. 'You can see that.'

'Which probably indicates that their losses are increasing,' Granny retorted.

'I heard from someone who speaks Japanese that they have received orders that if the Allies set foot on Honshu or Kyushu, their home islands, we are all to be eliminated and the guards then have to fall on their swords,' Grandpa said, with a certain relish.

'Bert, not in front of Ronald, please,' Granny said. Then turning to me, 'Do not worry, nothing like that will happen. When we win the war we will go back safe to home.'

I was not sure whether to believe Granny or Grandpa, and also decided that my parents would be unlikely to tell me the truth as Mum was of the opinion that I might repeat the comments where they could be overheard. I mused on the thought of Japanese falling on their swords. After all, King Kong had threatened to do it often enough. But I would not be around to see it if they killed us all first. King Kong had finally left, and we were almost sorry because he was quite a character, although officious and noisy. The old order was changing.

Roger was now only a couple of months off four years old, and he and his American friend Charley no longer stayed so close to home to play. Roger was now allowed to wander over part of the camp, but never to cross Main Road. There were no cars so he ran no risks from vehicles except the honey cart, and that came only once a day, and was pushed by four men. He used to enjoy playing near the sports field, as he knew the way there. That had been the scene of the Mauser pistol episode. Furthermore, he had often to go there for roll calls. He and his friend Charley had a passion for anything that moved. They loved insects and creatures that were alive. His favourite trick was a plot to give Mum hysterics. He would trot into the hut in his much patched sun-suit, with shorts as bottoms and a bib front with straps. Mum had made several out of a pair of curtains. Then, just as Mum was getting him to sit down and eat, he would reach into his bib front and produce a live toad and put it on the table. The result was always the same: Mum would skip out of the hut and shout 'Do something, somebody!'

The toads were, I suppose, five inches across, ugly, greyish muddy brown in colour with what seemed like warts on their bodies. They walked rather than hopped. Mum was terrified of them. Roger would think it great fun, but I was the one who generally had to remove them from the hut.

Our food was so sloppy and thin now, there was little to chew on. Flour, if it came, was of very poor quality, heaving with weevils, but at least they died when the flour was cooked. The bread issued was usually black, and of course full of those dead weevils. This type of food did nothing for Roger's developing jaw muscles, and Mum got quite worried as he was forever dribbling. Dr Grice tried to reassure Mum that given a proper diet his jaw muscles would recover and develop normally.

I and a dozen of us were fooling around on Main Street during the first week of August 1945, enjoying a bit of shelter from the sun under the avenue of acacias, as over the last week the weather had been unbearably hot. Some of the older inmates joined us. A nineteen-year-old Greek called Aliosa Martinellis swaggered into the group, intent on climbing a 60-foot acacia tree.

When he was nearly halfway up we shouted, 'Don't go any higher as the branches could snap.' He totally ignored us and kept climbing; then, suddenly, I heard a very loud crack, a yell and then a loud thump not far from my feet.

Peter went to check, and shouted to Brian: 'Go and get a doctor.' Meanwhile all Martinellis' clothes were slowly turning red with his blood. A door was acquired to serve as a stretcher. The number of onlookers was growing, for the overall noise had attracted a lot of people. The women started shrieking, and half a dozen men slid their hands under the body and lifted it six inches while the door was slid under. Dr Grice arrived and escorted the 'stretcher' to the hospital.

The Committee descended on us boys, but for once we were defended by the ladies, who confirmed that we had been trying to warn the boy, shouting 'Do not climb the acacia' ... 'Don't go any higher.' The fickleness of North

China acacias, particularly after a very hot spell, had been drummed into me from the age of six at least, and in the interests of self-preservation I had always heeded those warnings. When I got back to the hut for lunch I was not hungry, an unheard-of occurrence, and Mum thought I was sickening, but when I told her what had happened she understood and did not press me. Granny then came in to share the news; all I remembered from the accident itself was something that sounded like a bag of rice falling down ten feet away. Martinellis never recovered consciousness and he died that evening of awful internal injuries.

***

Ted McClaren told the Committee that Russia had declared war on Japan on 9th August, and he would try and get something definitive out of Watanabe, who was supposed to be the liaison person; then rumours started to fly around that the war was over, that we might be rescued … or that the guards were going to kill us all.

Mrs Lawless died of typhoid on 8th August, and as the graveyard was now full the burial the next day had to take place outside the walls, hence only a handful of people could attend. Watanabe was nowhere to be seen. He was tracked down and Ted McClaren tried to speak to him, but Watanabe just ran away, pursued by a few dozen inmates. They lost him when he fled through the front gates, knowing that the internees could not follow there. Watanabe was unpopular with the prisoners, but if he were behaving like that then surely there must be something to hide. What was it? Speculation grew wilder and wilder. I kept remembering Grandpa's predictions and wondered if we would all be killed before we could be freed from the camp. On 14th

August we had a special roll call on the sports field, and I eyed the machine guns in the towers. They traversed over our heads but nothing fired.

The next day there were more rumours that the Emperor of Japan had made a proclamation. Mum heard from Mrs Grice that Dr Vio had told her husband that the Emperor had given a broadcast, 'For the first time in 2,600 years Japan had to seek peace from four countries.' Was it really true? Nobody knew. The guards were conspicuous by their absence, but the answer was not long in coming.

12

Freedom from the Poached Egg

On the morning of 17th August I was down by the Church when the drone of an aircraft could be heard. A lot of people rushed out of No. 1 Kitchen and streamed towards the sports field. Suddenly a large American aircraft appeared from the sky and began to circle the camp. With each circuit it came lower, and out of the rear dropped seven parachutists. From the church-yard we were the nearest, so we ran down the sloping road and out of the gate, turned left and along the road to the end of the camp wall. The guards made no attempt to stop us. The Americans landed in a field of kaoliang, and one had damaged his shoulder falling on a grave mound. As we approached, the paratroopers emerged from the six-foot-high kaoliang with guns at waist height. On slipping out of their parachute harnesses they had put their fingers on the triggers of their carbines. When they realised that they were being approached by schoolboys, women crying with joy, and gangly thin men they relaxed. Explanations followed and they said that they had been briefed that the landing could have been opposed by the Japanese. It may well have been so, but the fact that the inmates rushed the gates without fear had not been a scenario anticipated by the guards. So they had just opened up the camp.

One of my friends grabbed at a parachute and we passed the silk around. 'Let's cut it up and each have a piece,' Peter said quickly.

'We could ask the soldiers to sign it,' I suggested eagerly, grabbing a piece of parachute silk, for to have autographs would be really exciting and a great coup. 'Anybody got a knife?' One appeared and the panels of the parachute were soon mutilated, and our heroes asked to sign before they disappeared into the camp. 'Please sign your name,' I asked the first officer I came to, held up my piece of parachute silk and he produced a stubby pencil. My friends were all doing the same thing. The good-natured soldiers obliged us, probably flattered to be asked and relieved to have such a happy friendly welcome instead of the hostile reception they had expected.

'Now don't you go tearing up any more of the parachutes, guys,' Major Staiger said as he scrawled his name on my piece of silk. 'One ruined chute is enough.'

'Yes sir,' we breathed as we trooped after them, mingling with the crowds. Not only did I get all seven signatures but acquired the pencil as well!

While this was going on the aircraft continued to circle, but now with its bomb doors open, dropping grey cylindrical containers, each with one parachute in a variety of colours. There had been one or two dropped with the parachutists, which they had immediately opened, and contained carbines and arms. Now things were more relaxed we were asked to find the containers, as falling among the kaoliang they were easily hidden.

It was really impressive how far the aircraft and soldiers

had come, having taken off at five a.m. from Kunming, which was near the Burma border, with a refuelling stop at Xian at eight. They reached Weihsien at eleven a.m.

Ted McClaren took the Americans towards the camp entrance; here they met the Committee members and had an informal conference as they walked, when Major Staiger explained that his mission was a humanitarian one, to take care of the health and welfare of the internees. He had only seven men and taking over the full responsibilities of the camp was out of the question. He valued the Committee's thoughts.

Then it was through the gates to accept the surrender of the Commandant in his office near the guardroom, where the Japanese guards were cowering. Major Staiger stated that his 'Duck' team (all relief teams had code names) would administer the camp with the camp's Committee of Nine. Defence of the camp from the surrounding guerrillas would rest with the Japanese, as would the provision of food and fuel. The Japanese officials appeared confused by the situation, because such a scenario had not been envisaged by the Japanese planners. The local commanders felt themselves unable to make a binding decision but agreed to accept the directives 'temporarily'.

Mr Izu, the Commandant, kept asking what would have happened if the Duck Mission had failed. He got a stock answer: in that case a second much larger team would have been sent and that would certainly not have failed. Izu then seemed to accept that the Americans were here to stay, and though the subsequent conferences with the Japanese authorities may have been dilatory they were never openly hostile. Major Staiger mentioned that, as his men would be staying in the camp, the only suitable buildings were the Japanese Headquarters, so the Americans took these over while the Japanese officials returned to their living quarters. Cpl Orlich set up his radio equipment and suddenly we were in communication with the world. During the early after-noon, Mr Koga, Vice-Consul at Qingdao, who happened to be in Weihsien when the Duck Team landed, called in, and the whole purpose and authority of the Duck Team had to be explained again. The agreement of the morning was re-negotiated, Mr Izu pushing for the Americans to take full control, but this was not agreed.

The Committee had recruited a number of men to form a camp police force, if necessary; Dad was one, so he swapped stoking fires and went on rostered guard duties at the gate. We still got hot food from the kitchen, so I suspected that someone else was now a stoker.

Whilst walking back to the gate, I asked one of the para-troopers what sort of aircraft they had jumped from and where their base was. I was told that they had come from Kunming and the aircraft was a B24 'Liberator'. The real excitement was that we could run in and out of the camp, though the Committee ruled that the outside gates had to be closed at 7 p.m. when it was still light, probably to ensure that the odd Chinese could not get in. The ground sloped down in front of the main gates to a stream, and beyond that, heading right, there was a small Chinese village two miles away. The village huts there were of sun-dried brick, red tile roofs and windows glazed with oiled and hence translucent paper. The village had been mistaken for a drop zone and one of the containers had come right through the roof of a house, fracturing the skull of a boy of fourteen, so he was admitted to the camp hospital. I felt sorry for him because I knew what it felt like, having suffered a similar injury.

When I got back to our hut, I told Mum what had

happened and asked her to look after my precious piece of silk. She was most impressed that I had got all the signatures and promised faithfully to look after it. So much so that, over seventy years later, I still have it. The names of the Duck Team were Major Stan Staiger, Ensign Jim Moore USNR,[69] Lt Jim Hannon, Sgt Ted Nagaki (American 'Neisi' – Japanese interpreter), Eddie Wang (Chinese interpreter), Cpl Peter Orlich (radio operator) and Sgt Ray Hanchulak (medical orderly).

Everyone was so happy that we had been rescued from the sky and now the American Army was in charge. Even Grandpa was cheerful and delighted his prophecy of death for us and hari-kari for the Japanese had proved wrong. Although the Japanese surrendered quietly, it was discovered that they did indeed have orders to kill their prisoners had the main Japanese islands been invaded by the Allies, which had not happened because of the dropping of the two A-Bombs on Hiroshima and Nagasaki.

We learnt that Major Staiger had deliberately left his parachute unfurled when he landed, as a check-point for further drops, and I now understood his comment about damaging parachutes.

The next day Major Staiger carried out an inspection, with Sgt Hanchulak and the camp doctors, and they decided that twelve inmates were in such poor health, physically or mentally, that they should be evacuated on the B24, which was expected to land that afternoon. But at the airfield the Japanese garrison, 200 army personnel, took up combat positions, so parachute panels were laid out to tell the airplane not to land but rather go back to Xian. The twelve patients, who had been moved to the airfield in two Japanese trucks, with Dr Grice as escort, returned to the hospital.

Major Staiger wanted Izu to explain what had happened

at the airfield. The Consular Commandant stated that the airfield belonged to the Japanese Army and that he had no control over them. Major Staiger then requested a message be sent from him to the Army Commander, and that he had no respect from an army whose officers did not obey orders. This upset the face of the local commander, Colonel Jimbo. So the next day he arrived at Weihsien. Ted McClaren and Major Staiger soon realised that the negotiations would be carried out at a different level. Mr Koga and Mr Izu were asked to withdraw. Colonel Jimbo went to great pains to explain that the US Government had not notified Tokyo of the intended descent on Weihsien. He asked that Major Staiger request that General Wedemeyer inform the Japanese Government of the authority of the Duck Mission. The protocol having been thus disposed of, the conference could get down to talk of the specific issues. Major Staiger told Colonel Jimbo that, in order to carry out his duties, he needed to get free passage of US aircraft at the airstrip. Col Jimbo agreed that American aircraft would be given full permission to land.

On 20th August Major Staiger discovered that the 'Eagle' mission had arrived in Weihsien city and was under the protection of General Li Wen Li of the Chinese Army. Contact was made with Colonel Byrd, US Army, and the Eagle Mission came out to the camp to inspect what had been done and to take photographs of the camp and internees. The next day the Dakota C47, which had brought the Eagle Mission, returned to Xian carrying Col Byrd.

In the next few days the administration of the camp was sorted out. As there was no information when the inmates would be evacuated, the first flush of freedom was somewhat dampened. The biggest local problem to solve was motor transport, to get to or from the Japanese-built airfield. The Japanese Army had four charcoal-burning trucks, two of which were always being repaired. Someone had found two pre-war Ford Sedan cars but there was no petrol for them, until the American Army agreed to provide some.

On 27th August a B29 Superfortress arrived from Okinawa, dropping leaflets to say that in one hour more B29s would arrive. Just before the arrival of the B29s a B17 Flying Fortress landed unannounced. This was full of photographers and news reporters after a story. Major Staiger did not permit them into camp, because their arrival had upset the delicate relationship between Major Staiger, Colonel Jimbo, the Japanese and the internees. I overheard Mum and Dad discussing the issue of the two groups of Americans and the three sources of aircraft-dropped supplies: the consensus was that the left hand did not know what the right was doing.

While this was being sorted out, the B29s from Okinawa arrived, bomb doors open. Their method of supply dropping was to fit a wooden grid, holding about fifteen containers, across the entire bomb bay. The containers themselves were made by welding together two large round 50-US-Gallon fuel drums. Two lugs were then welded on and a parachute fastened. The bombardiers aimed at an approximate corner of the camp, released the wood grid, which then fell with a single parachute. The oil drums followed and their parachutes jerked open, but usually ripped the lugs off. So effectively they became black cylindrical bombs, which hit the ground vertically and buried themselves half in the earth. The only way of opening one was by hacking off the top with an axe and trying to extricate something edible from the mix of cardboard boxes, tins of mixed soups, Spam, fruit and fruit juice. Major Staiger reported back that 25 per cent of the supplies were going to waste.[70]

By mid-September, while the B29s were making a hash of delivery, a B24 came in from Xian and made a perfect demonstration of how a dropping operation should be conducted, hitting the DZ marking panel squarely in the middle. The camp inmates and the Duck Mission spent the rest of that day and part of the next salvaging what they could from the B29 drop and distributing the goods.

Two C47 Dakotas arrived just after the mass drop. They left the next day, one carrying the twelve invalids and the other the rest of the Eagle Mission. However, they left Tech Sgt Willis, a communications expert from Georgia, behind at Weihsien. No parachute supplies came in for a couple of days, and during this time I was down by the main gate when Tipton and Hummel returned to the camp. I overheard them talking to two of the US Army personnel, describing the local situation. Then they went on to tell their former internee friends that the situation was mostly unsettled and that there was fighting between the Guomindang Nationalists of Chiang Kai-shek and the Ba Lu Jun of Mao Tse-tung's Communists. They were not very popular with their alarmist talk. By the same token, they were fed up by their reception in the camp; they were banking on a hero's welcome. Then they found that the US Army would not let them out of the camp, as they had still been on the Japanese roll of camp internees (the Commandant had not admitted very clearly that there had been an escape, because he would have lost 'face'). It was a strange situation but the US Army considered that, as they were now responsible for the whole camp, that was that. The Chinese friends of the onetime escapees were allowed to return to the guerrilla army.

A week after the first drop from B29s they started dropping supplies every other day, with B29s alternating from Okinawa and Saipan. They still used oil drums but welded the lugs on better so that they did not snap off. However, the aim was still as poor and several huts in the camp suffered 'bomb damage' from oil drums filled with tinned Del Monte peaches or Campbell's soup. In addition to food we started getting American khaki summer uniforms and boots or shoes. Initially only large sizes, but then I snapped up a pair of shiny brown polished boots in my size. Most of the boots were dull green-brown suede. Being young, agile and fairly fit, although still underweight, we could run faster to the spot where a parachute had landed and got there before the local farmers, who somehow thought it was all manna from heaven for them.

Very soon the recovery of goods became highly organised: us boys had to find the tell-tale fallen parachute, showing where the supplies had dropped within the kaoliang, and then guard it until the adults came to retrieve the contents.

Our ability to speak Chinese fluently was one of the main reasons we were allowed out of the camp. We were checked in and out at the main gate. On 'supply days' we used to spend most of the day seeking out those parachutes. A sort of code developed: if we got to a parachute first we kept it for the 'heavies' to empty, and the Chinese farmers did not interfere; but if they made it first we sometimes still got some of the contents, but only after they had looked it over. Cigarettes they took but chocolate bars they left.

More US Army personnel arrived at the beginning of September, and they brought additional clothes. They were commanded by Lt Col. Weinberg, who gave a 'pep talk' as to what should happen in the next few weeks. Captain Ashwood followed the Colonel and said that we were to be processed and orientated. We were to be re-indoctrinated, and adults needed to make an individual five-year plan. As a closing remark, he confirmed that he would be organising the programme himself. The Captain was of medium height and dark, and some women said he had Hollywood looks, but he was not popular with the majority. 'Hollywood Gasbag' was the preferred epithet: no one was used to a man who droned on and on about re-indoctrination and the importance of having a personal plan. Such irrelevancies did not endear Captain Ashwood to his audience.

On our way back from the sports field, I asked Mum what it all meant: 'What is orientation? And re-indoctrination? I want to know.' Fearing that this was leading up to yet another discussion of when and if ever I would go to school.

'I think he was telling us, in a roundabout way, that we have to learn all that has happened in the world while we have been here in camp,' Mum snorted. 'We need to be brought up to date on events and told about what they think will happen in the world in the next few years.'

'Have we missed much, Mum?'

'Probably,' Mum told me sighing, 'But we don't know yet, until we hear what Captain Ashwood has to say.'

'Do I have to come?'

'I don't think so. The Americans are organising all this and it is their idea of coming to terms with the changes. You need not worry about it.'

Relieved, I took her at her word and stopped thinking about orientation and re-indoctrination. Most of the adults did attend some of the talks over the following few weeks. They learnt from Capt Ashwood that England had had to give up all her Concessions in China, but didn't add that it was because of America pressure.

I and my friends preferred to go out of the camp and search for parachutes. The food from the drops was being issued to all of us and many people got sick from eating too much rich food. One particular soup, labelled 'Navy Bean Soup', was a thick yellow; it was very rich and had quite an effect on me, not that I ever vomited, but after trying some for several meals I gave it up. There were lots of other things to choose, like Del Monte canned peaches, and I tasted fruit salad for the very first time.

Now and then, when three or four of us were out scavenging, we came across containers inside the oil drums that had burst, mixing up all the contents. The B29 drops were particular culprits for this. If we were out of sight we used to select tins from the spilt rations and have a picnic, rather than return to camp for lunch. The rations had strange names, like 'C', 'D', and 'K', and there were even cardboard cases full of tins of Coca-Cola, but we learnt to avoid 'Root Beer', which had a vile taste. It was great fun sitting round the crater that the container had made having a secret lunch.

One day after the picnic lunch we had drifted off about two or three miles, finding ourselves near to a neighbouring village. There was a lot of noise and many Chinese milling about, so we went off to investigate. Worming our way through the crowd we came across a clearing in the middle of the village. Three graves had been dug in the ground, and about two dozen armed guerrillas stood around three Chinese men, who were kneeling. The wrists and ankles of the captives were shackled with barbed wire, with their arms behind their backs, again tied with barbed wire at the elbows, and with a piece of wood looking like a lavatory seat round their necks with writing on. I could not read the Chinese so I asked an intelligent-looking Chinese man what the characters meant. He told me the men had been stool pigeons of the Japanese and the Ba Lu Jun had tried them and found them guilty. After a bit more haranguing the three were made to kneel in front of the holes with a soldier standing behind each. These took their Mauser machine pistols, fitted the stock and stuck the muzzle of the gun on the middle of the skull. At a shouted order the three triggers were pulled. They must have been using dum-dum ammunition – the top of the human skull hinges forwards in such circumstances, and the victim topples into the prepared grave. I had heard tell of the summary executions of people deemed prisoners, but had not before seen it occur. The indifference of the Chinese crowd, who then dispersed, lived with me for weeks. But the incident confirmed that human life was cheap in China. I and the few boys that had seen the incident made our way back to Weihsien, agreeing that we must not shout about what we had seen. Because, we reasoned, if our parents found out then future expeditions out of the camp would be prohibited.

Apart from food, the drops included medicines, toothpaste and toothbrushes. Mum was delighted to get the latter: she carefully taught Roger how to use them but was less than amused when I admitted that I had forgotten how to clean my teeth properly. The problem was the only tap with 'safe' water was outside the men's showers, and that was over a quarter of a mile from our hut.

Always good business people, the Chinese started to come out of Weihsien city and set up stalls just outside the gate. They did a huge trade in fresh vegetables and fruit; fortunately the US Army had brought Chinese money to distribute amongst internees. Mum used to rave that she could finally get some fresh tomatoes: the parachute drop had supplied Heinz Ketchup, which was all very well, but not a patch on a sun-ripened tomato ketchup from California that she used to buy in Tianjin.

To reinforce his lectures Captain Ashwood had arranged for loudspeakers to be rigged up all over the camp. The internees did not think much of the testing one afternoon. The next morning the speakers burst forth at 6 a.m. with *'Oh, What a Beautiful Mornin', Oh what a Wonderful Day'*, followed by more Rodgers and Hammerstein, interspersed with remarks by Captain Ashwood, and this carried on all day. Ted McClaren requested that the speakers be silenced, but was told these broadcasts were on army orders and necessary for our re-indoctrination into the post-war world. The US Army personnel were most surprised, on the second morning when they turned on the speakers, that total silence reigned over the camp. The radio technicians were sent for, and they found that each speaker had one wire unscrewed, thus neatly sabotaging the US Army Broadcasts. The internees had no intention of letting the US Army disturb their peace, any more than they had allowed the Japanese to wear down their spirit during the war. The speakers were reconnected and Col Weinberg made a short broadcast saying: 'OK, I get the message. We will cease music broadcasts and the six a.m. transmissions, and other than essential messages we will transmit only the daily news at six p.m.'

Then one of the American soldiers developed scarlet fever, which upset the doctors. They isolated him, with two other people with whom he'd been in close contact, and got a US Navy plane from Qingdao to evacuate them. It all added to the daily excitement. The routine was something new, and things seemed to change every day.

The next day Ted McClaren announced that he was one of six men – all essential to the Tianjin business scene – who had been selected to fly to Tianjin the following morning in a B25.[71] Dad was also one of that group, so Mum was to stay with Roger and me. I was told that the plan was we would go by train to Tianjin over the following weeks. We were treated to a lecture on the sports field on the situation in England and in China. Extraterritoriality had been given away by the Americans in 1944. The British could not go back to their old way of life, which was gone forever.

England was broke and times were hard, even though we had been on the winning side. The situation in China was unsettled. The truce between the Guomindang and the Ba Lu Jun had ceased when Japan was defeated. Nobody could guess what would happen in the future.

At last the trains started running to Qingdao. First to be evacuated was the Chefoo School, 200 boys and girls and their teachers. Then all those going directly overseas from China. Five hundred and eighty people left early on a Tuesday morning for Qingdao. The next day those still sick were taken from Weihsien to the train to Qingdao. The camp was pretty empty now, except for those wanting Tianjin or Beijing. Rumours abounded, but it seemed to boil down to the fact that the railway was no longer secure. Anyway, we had to amuse ourselves – we could not just sit around and read.

The five rows of electric barbed wire fence around the outside of the camp had been dismantled when the parachute supplies arrived, and now the single strand along the top of the wall was taken off, which opened up opportunities for boyish adventures. It started with a dare. I don't remember who accepted the first challenge. But we climbed up on the wall near the main gate and the Church and walked past the sports field to the watchtower in the corner. At first that was a great triumph: the wall was about 18 inches thick, topped with a single-width brick of only 4½ inches, and hence it took a good sense of balance to get started, and then we had to step over the electrical insulators every six feet or so. Then I discovered that one could get around the tower and carry on along the wall southwards until reaching the first block. The tower there was impassable. One day I was running along the wall towards the Church when, jumping over an insulator, I missed my footing and fell off outside the wall, which was fifteen feet high. Luck was with me as a farmer had piled a lot of manure and straw on my impromptu landing zone. Thus I enjoyed a soft landing, albeit a smelly one.

As I crawled out of the cow muck, I was greeted with 'Poo. Don't come back like that, Bridge! Keep your distance.' I made a rude gesture in their direction, then ran off across the field and jumped into the stream to wash off the muck. The water was not much cleaner, as it was downstream from the village there. But at least I was not covered with brown and green slime and straw anymore. By the time I had run a few more lengths of the wall my clothes had dried. I decided that I smelt reasonable enough to go off back to my hut room.

Mum greeted me with the news that it had been decided that, as the railway line north had been blown up again and the trains were being attacked by the Communist guerrillas, we would be flying to Tianjin. First, though, the bomb craters in the runway had to be repaired using Japanese Army soldiers, so that took another week.

Those for Beijing were the first to go; they left the camp early in the morning, but they did not fly out until four in the afternoon. There was a great fuss about this, and reconnaissance planes kept coming overhead, checking on the guerrillas we supposed.

Two hundred more left on Monday 15th October, and we, as a family, were still in camp. All our activities had lost their glamour. All I wanted was to get off on a plane and join Dad and get to our old home as soon as I could. Mum and my grandparents had packed up our more precious things into our surviving trunks and even cardboard boxes, but because of the state of the railway this 'heavy baggage' was going to Qingdao to be taken by sea to Tianjin by the US Navy.

They apparently had stacks of landing craft milling around, originally for 'Operation Olympic'; the invasion of Japan that hadn't happened.

Finally, our turn came on 17th October, two months to the day after we had been liberated. Mum, Roger, my grandparents and I were now going by air. We were woken by a bell at 4.30 a.m. and had breakfast, then the trucks arrived at 6.30. As there were only four of them, they were going to do a shuttle, starting at 7.00 a.m. It was a strange feeling to be leaving the camp at last: these walls had been our home for the past two and a half years. I still remembered the Tianjin home and Beidaihe quite clearly, but Roger had only known Weihsien Camp.

We bounced down the track to Weihsien city. The road had never been 'tarmacked' and the flurry of activity by the US Army on the rain-soaked ground over the previous few weeks had turned it into a rutted track. As the sight of the walls of the camp receded I began to think in anticipation of my first flight.

The airfield had been extensively repaired by the Japanese, as the US Army Air Corps had heavily targeted the runways earlier in 1945, when we had heard that distant drone of aircraft. The runway, being grass, had tended to muffle the actual explosions. Here were four or five C47s, most of them heavily camouflaged, belonging to the US Army Air Corps. However, one was all shiny silver, polished aluminium, belonging to the US Marine Corps (USMC), and I was rather envious that my friends got to travel in that one. All the aircraft had seats along the length of the fuselage, either a metal bench-type, or canvas bucket seats by the windows.

We bounced along the grass runway and were soon airborne, climbing to 8,000 feet. Some of the women were screaming with fear as the aircraft left the ground. Half an hour later we crossed the coast, heading north over the sea, with the Shandong coast on the portside.

Roger, sitting next to Mum, shouted out with glee: 'Mummy, what has that lady got a bucket for?' … followed by 'Oh, Mummy look at that lady's breakfast!' The exchange made a few more ladies 'green'.

13

Back to Tianjin and Beyond

T he aircraft made a perfect landing at Tianjin airfield, which I worked out was east of the city near the old French Arsenal where, in what seemed a lifetime ago, I used to be taken to watch Uncle Harold ride in point-to-point races, which he usually won.

Dad had managed to get out and meet us. He had a large car with a US Marine driver, the vehicle allocated when he had arrived weeks before in the B25 Mitchell. We piled in and within the hour were back in the Court Hotel. It was two and a half years since I had last set foot in the building. Most of the servants were still there and turned out to greet us. They had been able to continue working under the control of a Japanese manager, who seemed to have turned one of the bathrooms in our flat into a sort of waterproof swimming pool. When I asked why, Mum explained that the Japanese did not get into a bath to wash; rather, if it was big enough they climbed in for a soak, but otherwise stood outside the bath and splashed water over themselves, using some soap between the splashing.

During the first few days I had to get used to having so

much space, such a change from our cramped quarters in Weihsien. Suddenly I had a bedroom to myself again. I did miss my friends, who had gone their separate ways; some with their parents had gone on home-leave to England, before being posted to another part of the Far East. Whilst Dad had recovered all the property that Pottinger and Co. owned and managed, he had no one to leave in charge to go back to England, and Mum did not want to leave him. From his letters we had gathered that Uncle Harold would arrive in April at the latest.

In early December Harold turned up, dressed in his British Army Colonel's uniform. He expected to be released from the British Army in March, and would be able to take over as the Director the following April. This would allow our part of the family to take a ship to England, via Hong Kong, in May, arriving in the UK in July, but it would mean that I would not get to Beidaihe that summer. The procedure to get passage on ships to England had started immediately. The UK arrival in July would allow six clear months before my parents, Roger and I could return to Tianjin early in the New Year of 1947, allowing Harold to go to Victoria, British Columbia to catch up with his wife. Roger could start school in January 1946 when the Tianjin Grammar School opened the lower forms. The only school teaching in English to twelve-year-olds was the Marist Brothers, St Louis College, but they only had vacancies for the new school year, and their school year started in September. I was, therefore, excused school before our departure to England. A simple plan that was to go so wrong.

Mum, meanwhile, was more intent on recovering our furniture and effects. The furniture in the hotel flat was mainly intact, and although worn was still useable. She went round to Bryners, and was assured that the goods in the packing cases and furniture were still safe. She arranged for the coal to be removed and the goods were taken round to the Court Hotel. The largest piece was an upright Chappell piano, which had belonged to my paternal grandfather, Albert Henry Bridge, and had been buried by him during the Boxer Rebellion of 1899 in Weichen, and then dug up four years later; it passed to Dad after my grandfather died, and all the Bridge children, except for me, learnt on that instrument. Emerging safe, intact and useable, it was finally lost to the Chinese Communists in 1954.

The salvaged linen took a lot of washing, Mum would not use bleach because of the delicate colours of the finely woven material. One other silk item that had not been touched was Grandfather Bridge's mandarin coat, to indicate the rank he had been awarded by order of the Empress Cixi in January 1903, which survives to this day. It is slightly damaged, in that in 1919 Aunts Freda and Jessie had each taken two exquisite jade buttons to make earrings, and I think they had been lost in the passage of time. The hat had always been missing, according to Dad.

Tianjin was so different now. The US Government had shipped in the entire Third Amphibious Corps, totalling over 50,000 US Marines, from Okinawa. The General commanding accepted on behalf of the Chinese Government the surrender of 50,000 Japanese military stationed in North China. These American marines were sent up to protect the railway line from Qinhuangdao to Beijing and the Tongshan coal mines from sabotage by Japanese, who were still lurking around, and from destruction by the Communists.

Mum was walking one day along what was Victoria Road, now Chieh Fang Pei Lu, to the shops when a Jeep screeched up beside her and an American voice shouted 'Margot!' Mum turned to find it was General Shepherd, commander of the 6th Marine Division, who had known Mum when he had been a Captain in the US Marine Legation Guard in Beijing in 1927–29, before Mum was married. My parents saw General Shepherd several times and, when Dad was asked about 'transportation', Dad replied that he had a car on order but did not know when he would get it. My parents got the immediate offer of the use of a Jeep and driver when needed.

Mum had not forgotten about Roger's dribbling and he was taken to see a paediatrician from the Mayo Clinic, who was masquerading in US Navy uniform. He confirmed Dr Grice's diagnosis, and prescribed chewing gum, but added the stricture to avoid Spearmint, because it created more saliva. Roger came away with boxes that seemed to contain hundreds of packets of Juicy Fruit and Cinnamon gum.

On the Bund side of the hotel property, the USMC had leased a warehouse from Dad, and it was used by the Fleet Post Office for the marines. I befriended the men stationed there and spent many a long hour talking with them. I suspect civilian boys in the presence of bags marked US Mail would have earned censure from some quarter, had it been known, but the attitude was then that 'the war is over, let's relax.' Mum gave the marines involved Yenching embroidery for them to send to their parents. On more than one occasion I went to the movies at the USMC Post Exchange Theatre, riding there in a US Mail Jeep.

With no school in prospect Grandpa took over teaching me electrics, physics and maths. By February, with the air warmer, looking out of the flat I could see that there were a dozen or so LCM-6s tied to the Bund. These were just over 40 foot in length and had a 14-foot beam. They had had their twin 50 calibre machine guns removed and were manned by a crew of two or three. I saw them pottering all over the river, so one day I went down and talked to the crews. I found that they had two diesel engines, two propellers, no rudder but were steered by using the throttles. After about a week of scrounging rides, I was offered a chance to steer one. The sailors were, I suppose, boat happy as they would soon be going back to America. Before long I was happily 'driving' these LCM-6s up and down the river.

News came through that the British Army were not going to release Uncle Harold until June, so all the arrangements and boat bookings for a passage to England were deferred. This meant that we could go to Beidaihe after all. The trains were running so it was out to Tianjin East Station on a Thursday in June 1946, although this time in a USMC Jeep, and those first-class carriages on the train were just as comfortable as I remembered from six years before.

One thing I did notice was that there were far more watchtowers along the route of the rail track. These seemed to be manned by USMC personnel, with a few Nationalist soldiers as well. Tongshan Station was much the same, although sticky apples were not for sale this time, and then on to Beidaihe Junction, where we found that the train to Beidaihe was no longer running, but there were trucks with seats to take us the last twenty miles or so.

The houses were the same and we were soon settled in the double-storey house, which always had a gentle breeze flowing through the upper floor. Swimming and messing around with small boats off the beach was the same as I remembered it. Suddenly the three weeks were over, although Dad had interrupted his time with a trip back to Tianjin. We retraced our steps on the journey back, but this time at Tongshan there was indeed a vendor selling sticky apples, so I could indulge once more.

On both the journey north and then south I had noticed a

number of General Motors 1½ ton trucks belonging to the USMC, with wheels modified to run on the railway line, and they were obviously used to patrol the railway line because the Ba Lu Jun (the 8th Route Army or Communist Forces) were constantly trying to blow up the line and the USMC were trying to prevent it happening. In a way the train ran through warring factions, each with their own agenda, and never mind the populace. Arriving back in Tianjin I found that the US Navy had pulled most of its LCMs away from Tianjin, so that was my fun on the water over with.

The Bund, though, was alive with activity, UNRRA[72] supplies being unloaded as aid to China, though the majority were left on the dockside, where the tins rusted, the contents perished, the clothing rotted, and the machinery got stolen. I will always remember the cases and cases of turkey breast to feed the hungry, when what the population wanted was wheat or rice. The sports equipment given by the benevolent Uncle Sam was rusting away whilst the people wanted the necessities of life.

Almost daily, a pathetically rusty Japanese-owned coaster, which barely looked safe enough to cross the river, was loaded up with hundreds of Japanese civilians. They sailed down the river and across the China Sea to a Japanese port. I thought at least when we were sent to Weihsien we used a train, but we had not needed to cross the China Sea. These little coasters were all the Japanese had left from their quite substantial merchant fleet of 1941.

Dad came home towards the end of July with definitive bookings, the late-August passage to Shanghai via Qingdao was to be on the MV *Wanhsien*, a converted Landing Ship Tank[73] of 4,000 tons, owned by UNRRA,[74] who had hired the experienced China coast captains formerly with Butterfield & Swire or Jardine Matheson. Then we were due to leave Shanghai in early September, on Cunard's RMS *Britannic*, which had been converted to a troopship and was being used to transfer the British Army back to the UK from all over the Far East. Former civilian internees were granted passage through the bureaucratic machinations of the Ministry of War Transport in London.

We duly embarked on the MV *Wanhsien*, and sailed down the Hai River. The lower tank deck was packed with UNRRA supplies as there was no more space for them in Tianjin docks, the open upper deck with Chinese deck passengers. The ship did not have the anti-pirate guards that were usual on the China coast and we and others had cabins in the rear. The passage to Shanghai was uneventful, other than bother about the toilets (or 'heads' using US Navy terminology), which were in a line across the rear of the cabin area, eight or ten standard European toilets. But there were no partitions, just a metal hand rail between each toilet bowl and no means of privacy. A sign hung on a bit of string on the door, marked MEN on one side and WOMEN on the other, to be turned as necessary, did not prove very effective as no one bothered to read the signs. The Captain took a command decision and by the time we had reached Qingdao the toilet bowls were each surrounded by a six-foot plywood partition, complete with rickety door.

As we approached the Yangtze delta the seas got quite rough and a flat-bottomed landing craft, however large, was not the most stable of ships, and I was told the ship behaved rather like a cork in a bucket when we had to skirt a typhoon off the China coast. We took on the pilot and sailed up the Wangpoo River and approached the wharf and were soon ashore. My Uncle Alwyne had been the British Consul-General in Shanghai since 5th September 1945 and had arranged for a car to pick us up, as we were staying with them for the few days before the *Britannic* sailed for England.

When we got to the Consul-General's house with its secluded garden, not far from the International Bridge, Aunt Jessie was there to greet us but with bad news. The RMS *Britannic* had broken down in Singapore and our journey had been cancelled. Not only was shipping to the UK in turmoil, but in a week's time there was going to be no hotel accommodation in Shanghai, due to a UN Convention. Uncle Alwyne was expecting the British Ambassador and his entourage. Dad had had business dealings with Horace Kadoorie and the two were fellow dinner guests one night at Uncle Alwyne's. Dad explained the Bridge family predicament, and Mr Kadoorie said he knew their Palace Hotel was full of the UN people but he would get the Bridge family in the following month. Meanwhile why not come and stay with his family at Marble Hall, there were stacks of rooms and they were not expecting house guests until November? In the event we stayed at Marble Hall for three weeks, before coming back into the heart of the city with a suite at the Palace Hotel on the corner of the Bund and Nanking Road. Passage booking once again became the ritual. The reservation, when it came through, was in a month's time on Canadian Pacific's RMS *Empress of Australia*. Another four weeks to kill, and still no sign of school.

Then, with two days to go, panic: shipping plans changed, but fortunately not much. The *Empress of Australia* was running a day or so late, so to save time we were to embark on a sloop, HMS *Black Swan*, to be taken to the *Empress of Australia* and transferred at sea at the entrance of the Yangtze. It was a rough sea for the transfer: the passengers got across relatively easily by breeches buoy, great fun for a twelve-year-old boy, but when it came to the baggage the sea was rougher and one of Mum's trunks was dunked. Fortunately only for a few minutes, so not a lot of water got in. Mum was able to visit the baggage room on the *Empress of Australia*, open the trunk up and dry it all before we reached Hong Kong on 5th November 1945.

The Hong Kong shoreline was virtually untouched from the mid-1930s, the largest building being the 14-storey Hong Kong and Shanghai Bank building in the middle of Victoria, completed in 1934. We were met by Captain Leo Lamb, a lifelong friend of my parents in Tianjin, and enjoyed a tour of the island as well has some of Kowloon, against whose main pier we had tied up. The stay was all too short, then it was away again. This time to Singapore where my parents' best man, Major Archie Anand, met us in his Jeep and we had a short tour of the Botanical Gardens followed by tea at Raffles Hotel. It was a day-stop and the Captain was anxious to get on. We still had empty cabins, so next stop was Colombo. Here yet another pre-war friend, Major 'Peanuts' Way, who was still in the British Army, picked us up in his Jeep and took us to the Zoological Gardens, followed by lunch at Mount Lavinia Hotel which was on the beach just south of Colombo.

Then it was back to the ship. The next day, at sea, the tannoy announced that as the ship was full we wouldn't be stopping at Aden but would be going straight to Suez, entering the Red Sea at Perim Island. So to alleviate the boredom of crossing the Arabian Sea children's sports were on the menu. Roger looked forward to this but I was indifferent, almost in a 'Do I have to?' mood. They were duly held, with egg and spoon races, and deck quoits etc on the promenade deck.

We reached Suez as the sun was setting, picked up the pilot and then went through the Suez Canal at night. The next morning the ship moored in Port Said, and there was the entertainment of the gully-gully men, diving for coins and trying to sell souvenirs. Then the ship cast off again for our next destination: Malta. But when we got there the sea was running with quite a swell, and the ship too large to risk the narrow entrance. The Captain was advised by the Royal Navy Harbour Master not to try negotiating the passage through the narrow channel. The tannoy message to the passengers was quite simple: 'This is the Captain speaking. The sea is too rough, the wind too strong, next stop Liverpool.'

14

A Short Interlude in England

We passed through the Straits of Gibraltar at night, then found that the Atlantic was calm and forecast to be that way until Liverpool. The Captain took the ship relatively close to the Portuguese and Spanish coasts; passing Cape Finisterre I almost felt that, had we been a yard closer, I could have stepped ashore. The Bay of Biscay, despite its reputation for poor weather, was like a mill pond; then suddenly, at dawn, the north coast of Wales was off in the distance on the starboard side. I admit that I was getting quite excited.

The entrance to the Mersey hove in sight, the ship slowed to pick up the pilot, and it was not long before we were moored near the Royal Liver Building. I had managed to get a space by the deck railings so got a good view. For many, like me, this was the first sight of England, and others had not been in England for at least six years. Despite that there were endless queues, at English Customs and Immigration.

Home Office immigration officials had to have their pound of flesh. As Dad had been born in China, his father's birthplace became an issue, and as it was Glamorgan that seemed to be in order, but he was told that he would have to produce proof at a police station within seven days.

Mum seemed to sail through as she was born in Yorkshire, but then both Roger and I were on Mum's passport as additional children, yet we were born in a British Concession of a father born in China, but a paternal grandfather born in Glamorgan. It got too difficult for the immigration official so he referred us and our passports to the head of Liverpool Immigration. The outcome was that, even now in the 21st century, and seven passports later, when communicating with the Passport Office I have to quote: 'grandfather born Ferndale Glamorgan 1868'!

We then got on a train from Liverpool Lime Street Station to Rugby, via Crewe. The journey took three hours, and Mum's uncle, Jack Fleet, met us and took us to their house, which was on Hillmarton Road. Jack was Grandpa's brother and had owned and run a chemist's shop in Rugby. Mum's two cousins, Mrs Nestor Wiggins and Norman Fleet, lived with their respective husband and wife in nearby Dunchurch. Norman now ran the chemist's shop, having had a break in the RAF as a navigator on de Havilland Mosquito aircraft during the war.

Hearing of the food shortages in immediate post-war Britain, Mum had packed cases with tinned food. The restriction on baggage on the ship was volumetric, not by weight, and we had been allowed 40 cubic feet, nominally one ton per adult. Mum's aunt and uncle were concerned that Mum was planning on using their house as a base to visit other relatives and friends. For some reason her aunt was not pleased with this, and after some discussion we ended up staying through December 1946, having what in my view was a very pleasant Christmas, and then moved to the Bonnington Hotel in Bloomsbury, London. There we walked round the sights of London and we saw a couple of pantomimes.

Then we went to Plan B, as we could not go and stay with Mum's cousin in Yorkshire, or to army friends in Wales before February. So my parents decided to throw money at the problem and go and stay at the Studland Bay Hotel in Dorset. The journey down was uneventful, but two days later it snowed … and it snowed. In a couple of days we were snowed in. The news on the radio was a story of roads blocked and of farmers in Kent digging out sheep from 10-foot drifts.

It was not as bad in Dorset, but great fun as I had not seen such deep snow before. Making snowmen with Roger got a bit boring after ten straight days, and I was looking forward to Yorkshire, where my second cousins lived.

But first it was back for my birthday to be nearer the centre of things, and we moved to Moore Place Hotel in Esher. The next day it was up to London where we met up with my cousin Douglas at the Bonnington Hotel and all trooped off on 4th March to see Aunt Freda and Uncle Tullis off at Waterloo, where they were catching a train for Southampton and then RMS *Strathmore* to Hong Kong. I learnt that they were then hoping then to catch the SS *Hupeh* to Tianjin, arriving on 13th May.

Now from mid-March the county progress commenced. First we went off to Dolgellau in Wales to see some old army friends of my parents from the 1930s, and then by train via Chester, where much ceremony was going on at the station as Field Marshal Montgomery was 'naming' a railway engine at one of the platforms; then, after changing trains at Stockport, we reached Mirfield in Yorkshire to stay with Norman and Dorothy Hudson. Mrs Hudson was Granny Fleet's niece and hence a cousin of Mum.

The Hudsons had two boys: Norman a year older and Roger a year younger than I. We spent most of April there and I got on well with Norman. We had great times, especially on a neighbouring farm owned by a Mr Dugdale. He had a milk round and it was fun doing it with Norman. The Hudsons had a spare bicycle and I used that, though I did find the hills and valleys of Yorkshire's West Riding rather different cycling conditions than the flat area of Tianjin.

At the end of April Dad was getting nowhere over passages to the Far East. All sea journeys were still in the bureaucratic hands of the Ministry of War Transport, and they were at a loss to understand why a family wanted to go *back* to China. My parents decided that to get anywhere, even by letter, with the MoWT it had to be back to the London area. Esher was the favoured spot again, but this time it was Hill House Hotel, as Moore Place was full. After a London visit, the Government finally approved: the journey east was to be on the RMS *Empress of Scotland* leaving Liverpool 23rd May 1947. Thus, our brief visit to the UK was soon to be over.

Mum did not want me to stay on my own in England until the school year started in September, though I could not see that there was sufficient time to go out to Tianjin and then back again in time for boarding school. Part of Mum's reasoning was that there were no near relatives for me to stay with in the summer of 1947. I think that she had convinced herself of this before our very convivial visit to the Hudsons. Enquiries and a visit to Bedford Modern School got me down for entry in September 1948, which obviated the impossible rush of trying to do it all in 1947. The real reason for the delay to plans had been occasioned by Uncle Harold's late release from the British Army and then the lack of shipping between the UK and China.

Commercial flights were not yet scheduled between the UK and Hong Kong.

Thus on 22nd May 1947 we packed up in the UK, our baggage considerably less and much lighter than on arrival. Departing from Hill House we caught a train from Esher to London and then on to Liverpool, where we departed on the next day on the *Empress of Scotland*, still painted in her battleship grey and still under the control of the Ministry of War Transport and the Board of Trade. First stop was to be Port Said, where the Captain announced that as the ship was only half full and there were no passengers to be picked up or dropped off until Singapore, we would be sailing from Suez down the Red Sea and across the Indian Ocean to Singapore as the first stop.

The Suez Canal was negotiated, a brief glimpse of Perim Island at the south end of the Red Sea and then eastwards to Singapore, where we arrived on 14th June. We had a day stop during which we visited the Tiger Balm Gardens, where the statues were almost grotesque, and then it was a couple of days' sailing up to Hong Kong and goodbye to the *Empress of Scotland*. We had had an extraordinarily quick transit from Liverpool.

We moored on the Kowloon pier, then a short ride to the Peninsular Hotel, an imposing building overlooking the harbour. We stayed in the Peninsular Hotel until 28th June when we embarked on Butterfield & Swire's SS *Hupeh* for the journey up the China coast, missing out all of the ports to Dagu, where we took on the pilot for our transit up the Hai Ho River to Tianjin, arriving on 5th July 1947. The journey on the SS *Hupeh* had been interesting, with deck passengers isolated behind a barbed wire barrier and separated from the cabin passengers by armed Indian guards, ever watchful for attack or even attempts at ship boarding by Chinese pirates.

There were occasional sightings of threatening junks but they soon veered away when they saw the turbans of the Sikh guards and their Lee-Enfield rifles.

15

Back to the Old Routine

Then it was rapidly back to the conditions of my early childhood, except I fouled it up by going down with chicken-pox at the end of August. Harold and his wife Hilda, along with Aunt Freda, were in Beidaihe staying at the Bridge property. Harold had been travelling to and fro from Tianjin and reported that trains were erratic. So my chicken-pox was the excuse not to leave Tianjin for the summer of 1947, but as Mum said there would always be next year.

My schooling then came up as a rather pressing topic, I had realised for some time that the utopian sojourn of no schooling was bound to end sometime. Mum, I think, also felt insecure and did not want me to be removed from her immediate presence, and Dad seemed to be of the opinion that things could not get any worse. Whilst conscious of the status quo, I had tried in my own way to soak up knowledge. Grandpa Fleet was a mine of information about things electrical and mechanical. I was round at the local Chinese electrical workshop often. Similarly, I also spent long hours in the Court Hotel's carpenter's workshop, honing my woodwork, also learning to pick locks and cut keys. These skills all learnt in Chinese.

If you had asked me what my ethos had been over the previous six years it had been to watch, to question and to copy. That means of learning was about to change. I was taken to St Louis College in the former French Concession, a Marist Brothers institution on Rue St Louis. The Headmaster was Brother Kenny, a very intense Irishman, and a form/class was sorted out which was considered to be at right level for me. I found that languages other than English and Chinese were not my forte. My parents pointed out that it would only be for a year, as I was starting school in England in September 1948. The school catered for all nations and creeds: British, American, Russian, French, German, Chinese and every combination of them, but I was relieved to hear that tuition was in English.

The teachers at St Louis were mainly Irish, Spanish, French or German, but all were members of the Marist Brothers, a Roman Catholic teaching order. The local government decreed that all students had to have an 'Official' student marker, a metal enamelled badge so that they could be identified. The Headmaster rapidly designed a small red and yellow shield to be worn either on a coat lapel or on a sweater.

School in the mornings started with prayers: *Pater Noster, Credo, Ave Maria*. A break mid-morning, and then a *Gloria* and *Ave*, which was repeated at the start of each lesson throughout the day. A culture shock, but I got used to it, and it quadrupled my knowledge of Latin.

I started in September 1947 as soon as I was clear of chicken-pox. St Louis was a day school so I continued to stay at our flat in the Court Hotel, returning for lunch each day, as the Marists only provided a lunch of Chinese food, and

I think Mum was suspicious of its origin. So, I got on my bicycle and rode a little more than a mile each way for lunch. Four to five miles each day, and half that on Saturdays. There was usually a good hour of homework each day. Thus I was able to get some English reading in as well, and consumed Zane Grey and other cowboy epics. Through the next four years I was to get through Nordoff and Hall and Nicholas Monserrat, and dipped into some of Dad's John Buchan.

In October I was able to resume cycling round Tianjin. This was a joy in a way in that the steepest road slope was probably 1 in a 100, such a change from the hills of the Yorkshire Dales, as here the highest ground was the dyke containing the creek, which stank mainly of sewage. Road traffic was relatively sparse and the only normal hazards to riding a bicycle were three-wheeler pedicabs and the traditional rickshaw, two wheels and human powered, although an occasional open-air tradesman was inept at moving his portable stall and would wheel it with all his stock into the path of an approaching cyclist.

I mentioned this to Dad one day and he told me to avoid a collision at all costs, because in the event of an accident, especially with a European boy, the vendor would use it as an excuse to claim that all his stock had been contaminated, damaged or destroyed and seek substantial compensation.

It was for the same reason that Dad employed a chauffeur for his Ford V8; his Rover had never been returned by the Japanese Army. Any sort of accident meant the driver went to gaol while things were sorted out, which could take some time. Dad thus declined to drive himself, for obvious reasons.

The Country Club was not functioning due to refurbishment after the US Marines left, so in August I had to resort to using Parkes Road Swimming Club, and then bumbled along at school. Come the end of September thoughts of the annual play started exercising the teaching staff. Although the original play had been written in French, it was decided to use English. I was given a fairly major part as my English diction was quite understandable to all. The play was set in medieval times in an alpine castle. I learnt the part, now long forgotten, over the next six weeks.

Christmas 1947 came and went but by now the security situation was somewhat different and alarming. Tianjin was surrounded by the Communist Army and travel out of the city area was out of the question. Communication with the outside world was still possible by the river, which could take ships of 3 or 4,000 tonnes out via Dagu and then by sea to Shanghai and Hong Kong.

New Year was a dull affair as the city was surrounded by the Ba Lu Jun (8th Route Army) and travel was curtailed. Studies at school continued in 1948, and things looked as though they would work as planned. The political situation grew ever-more unstable, and so by July my planned return to England and Bedford School went by the wayside. But softball was on the agenda until the end of September 1948, when it got too cold and soccer became the game; the frozen ground to come in the winter precluded any other form of football. Dad told me that in the 1920s and 1930s they had ploughed the Minyuan field and then rolled it to ensure that ankles were not broken, and so allowed tackling and hence rugby flourished, but that was when there had been a British battalion to form an opposition, and considerably more rugby aficionados.

The school had only a city block and hence a small restricted sports field. Soccer was played seven a side, which seemed acceptable, and provided some sort of exercise. By the end of the month the sound of artillery had increased:

from occasional but sporadic to almost continuously and daily.

One of the chief obstacles was the Chinese yuan, which meant that your money was worthless outside of China. The Chinese dollar, which had been 16 to the pound sterling in 1940, had reached 60 million by the end of 1947. It was not uncommon to use bundles of notes of several million yuan tied with string and a paper seal with some bank's rubber stamp to certify the bundle contained x million yuan. It was pointless trying to go shopping with a wallet. To go shopping I just filled the saddle bags of my bicycle with cubes of bank notes of about four inches (10cm) each side.

The cold January heralded the New Year. At least there was central heating and as the railway to Tongshan still functioned, coal was available and physically we lived in relative comfort. Spring arrived on time and the double-glazed windows were removed and the fly screens substituted. By the end of April it was beginning to get quite warm. St Louis, after a brief frenzy of sports, settled into the routine of softball. There was a lot of equipment left to the school by the US Marines when they had returned to America from China.

Towards the middle of April I cut my knee, and it rapidly got infected; within days my left thigh had a huge swelling, especially in the groin where the gland was almost the size of a duck egg, and Dr Grice pronounced that sepsis (septicaemia) was evident. I was rushed by rickshaw to the hospital he had set up in the old British isolation hospital. Things were not looking good. He finally decided that an operation to drain the injury was necessary. But first he had a little bottle marked 'Penicillin', which he had been given by a US Navy doctor and which should cure the infection. The problem was the dose; anyway some was tried and by next morning the inflammation had diminished considerably and when the knee was lanced a basin of pus emerged. The stench reminded me of the fetid creek we crossed on the way to the Country Club. Another ten days and it was back to St Louis, but I had the luxury of a rickshaw for the first fortnight as the bandaged knee prevented cycling.

The Country Club swimming pool was still closed for essential repairs. Fortunately, the Parkes Road pool near the Recreation Ground was still open. Swimming was thus still possible. This pool, though, was slightly shallower and I hit the bottom diving in and lost a small piece of a front tooth, which is still missing. The summer continued with softball being played.

The Country Club fortunately had some 12-foot sailing dinghies so one could sail around the lakes surrounding the Club. Life was not too bad. The future was definitely in the 'too difficult' tray. Life had to be taken on a day-to-day basis. What was certain was that the travel conditions were such that Beidaihe was out for 1948. Mum decreed that for me to go off alone at the age of fourteen amid the present political situation to school in England was out of the question, thus I was destined to get my education al fresco at St Louis. I do not think anyone envisaged the events of the next three years.

St Louis and St Joseph's School started again in September, the routine no different to the previous year. Sport was again soccer, though I was looking forward to the next season's ice hockey. Towards the end of November 1948, artillery could be heard day and night. Nevertheless, the matting sheds were put up in the Minyuan in anticipation of flooding and freezing the ground for ice hockey. Little did anyone realise that this was a fruitless task.

Dad came home one evening to say that the last Butterfield

& Swire ship had departed, and that they did not think they would be operating for a few months. In effect we were going to be cut off, as China Airlines had also stopped flying its service to Shanghai some three months before. He then produced from a largish bag a 10ft x 5ft Red Ensign, saying 'I tried to get a Union Jack but this was the biggest flag they had on the SS *Hunan*. Ronald, we must check the rope on the flagpole on the Bund side of the hotel, because I think that we need to identify ourselves.'

So on a cold clear December day I shinned up the pole, checked the rope and the Red Ensign was duly hauled up. There it remained for nearly two months, though the rope got shot through and broke twice. As I climbed the mast the next time to effect repairs to the rope, I wished that I had nailed the flag up.

The next day when riding my bicycle to school I turned off what had been Victoria Road into Ewo Road to be confronted with a large shell crater, into which I went. I picked myself up and my bicycle, which had suffered a slightly twisted front wheel. Things were getting close. Having kicked the front wheel straight I carried on riding to St Louis. On getting home for lunch, I casually remarked that the roads were getting damaged by the shelling. Mum responded that she had noticed that when she had gone to Granny Fleet's for coffee, but that the rickshaw coped very well.

Life then went on as usual, and there was the odd end-of-term examination, in which I did well except for French and Religious Knowledge. The middle of December came and went with me doing two performances of the school play, which meant that then I could wash the script out of my brain. Meanwhile, outside school, preparations were in hand for Christmas. I realised that it was going to be a pretty tame affair, rather like Weihsien's Christmases had been. This time though, we would not even have the cama-raderie of camp: this was someone else's war, and we were just caught up in it.

The amount and frequency of the shelling increased, one could tell the 'crumps' of the 155mm guns and howitzers from the sharper barks of the 105mm guns. Nationalist soldiers could be seen on the streets; I did not envy them, as their ill-fitting uniforms seemed far too thin for the winter conditions soon to come. There was a big pitched battle just south of Beijing on 21st December, which the Nationalists lost, mainly because the Communists had acquired the Nationalists' ex-US Sherman tanks, which they drove over the frozen ground. However, in Tianjin the sounds of the guns seemed to be coming from the east and west of the city, rather than from the north or south; that was probably because the city was very much orientated north–south and one was nearer open country in our flat close to the river.

On 22nd December school was over and I did not have to ride my bike to school, so I went out walking to a shop almost opposite the Gordon Hall, with the innocent aim of buying some boiled sweets. Suddenly, salvo after salvo of 155mm shrapnel started bursting on the ground and scyth-ing over the street. My brain definitely said: 'You've to get out of this.' So in a lull, presumably while the gunners were reloading, I took to running from one tree to the next for the 200 yards towards the Court Hotel.

Soon after I came across a terrible sight, right in front of me. A Chinese woman in her twenties had tried to cross the road at a run, carrying her baby, when a shell exploded nearby. She kept going, but the baby's guts were spilt over the road and she tripped on the entrails, falling into the arms of a couple of passers-by on the other side of the street.

All my instincts were to help, but I was still 40 yards away from where she ended up, and I could see she had help from her own people, so against my better instincts I left her.

Suddenly the entrance to the Court Hotel appeared, a quick right turn and I'd be there, and at least I would be protected from the shrapnel. Up in our flat I described what I had seen, and Mum was visibly very shocked. Dad took me to the window, where I could see the Red Ensign flying from the flagpole, albeit rather smaller than when originally put up, as a month of wind, shrapnel and bullets had taken their toll. 'Ronald, you can see that they appear to be trying to miss the building, so the hunch worked, although the "red" of the flag is getting very "holed" with shrapnel.'

It had been a dramatic morning and I could see more trouble ahead: the issue of the Nationalists and Communists needed resolving, and only they could do it. Granny and Grandpa Fleet stayed the night on Christmas Day, at the Court. Inevitably, the conversation hinged to a large extent what was happening with the civil war, still obviously in full swing, and the conditions it brought. Tullis brought the news that Chen Cheng, the Nationalist (Guomindang) General in Tianjin, had managed to sell much of the weaponry, mainly 105mm and 155mm guns and ammunition provided by the Americans as 'aid' to bolster the Nationalist cause, to the Communist General Lin Biao, whilst Fu Zuoyi at Beijing was biding his time for a better price. Tullis had worked as an engineer at Woolwich Arsenal during the First World War and liked to think he was an expert in artillery matters.

To make up for the gap in Tianjin's defences three regiments had been borrowed from Fu Zuoyi, the General in command at Beijing. They were positioned in the former Italian Concession near the East Station, and in the former

Austrian and Japanese Concessions. The adults around me seemed remarkably relaxed about the prospect of being attacked by the Communists. Dad's view was that it would be worth their while. The level of corruption in the existing regime was such that it was felt that it would probably be the lesser of two evils to work with a brand new administration.

Dad also announced that he was very conscious of the threat to ordinary working Chinese, and he felt that he must do something for those who relied on him. The Hotel had about eighty rooms of which about fifteen were filled with Europeans, the rest empty. So Dad advised the hotel employees and the company office staff that they could come and stay in the hotel, which of course enjoyed the protection of the Red Ensign flying above. The staff were grateful because their dependants, especially the teenage girls, were, they feared, at risk from soldiery of either persuasion. Thus nearly 300 Chinese came to stay until the end of January. They had brought in all the food that they could lay their hands on and most of the baths were filled with water in case there was a shortage.

The amount of shelling did increase, and it seemed rather stupid to go round the streets, so I stayed in our flat. The scything of shrapnel was my major worry, compounded by the knowledge that I could not expect any medical assistance if hit. On the other side of the Hai Ho River there was also a Bund, which the Japanese had built during their occupation in the Second World War, with warehouses or godowns, and I could watch the Nationalist and Communist soldiers creeping along trying to hide from each other.

The Nationalist (GMD) soldiers were armed with a rifle and a leather pouch containing three 'stick grenades'[75] worn on their right buttock, except they had trimmed the pouch so that the handles of the grenades were easily grabbed then pulled out and thrown. The grenades also had small metal curtain rings tied on the end of the cord; the idea was that the soldier put his finger in the ring, and would then pull it when the device landed to ignite it. Running through the bushes meant that, at times, a ring got caught in a branch: about 10 yards and 5 seconds later there was a large bang and body parts were spread over the ground, or suddenly hanging from trees. If I saw it happen once, I saw it a dozen times.

The shelling kept up for ten days, and inevitably the Red Duster had to be fastened up again, but this time I had some help from the son of one of the members of staff. It was now only about 5 foot square; down to a Union Jack with a bit of red bunting underneath, but still it served its purpose.

Fighting in the outskirts of the city went on sporadically, but it was over within forty hours and the city then lay quiet. Mid-morning of 14th January saw the Communist forces flooding up from the south, along what used to be Victoria Road, led by former American Sherman tanks, which had obviously changed hands between the two Generals for a 'consideration'. The artillery and its ammunition had also been bought by the Communist General, despite being heavily marked 'For Mutual Defence', and no doubt the Nationalist General's Swiss bank account had benefited.

That afternoon I went out with Dad and the British Consul-General, Mr E. W. Jeffery. On the street all around us lay spent and live ammunition, abandoned weaponry, bodies and bits of bodies … in other words the usual detritus of battle, as we walked north along Victoria Road and Rue de France, both soon to be renamed North Liberation Street.[76] The fighting was continuing over the International Bridge and the Italian Concession, where the detached Beijing forces were deployed. Those three battalions on loan from Beijing kept fighting until the end of the month, when Beijing itself surrendered, and the areas they defended were reminiscent of the pictures of the siege of Stalingrad I have seen since. The Tianjin General Chen Cheng, having seen the hopelessness of the situation, had put down his baton on 15th January.

The first thing that struck me was the bearing and uniforms of the Communist soldiers. They were dressed in the usual North China winter clothes, piling layer upon layer of cotton padded clothing, making them look almost like Michelin Men. We came across about thirty men looking very dejected with their hands tied with barbed wire; they were short at least two if not three layers of clothing and their feet were in open rope sandals with bare toes showing. These Nationalist POWs were obviously almost frozen: the air temperature at midday didn't get above 20°F (-6°C).

It was also obvious that there were individual soldiers on both sides who were Japanese. Remnants of Japan's Kwangtung Army, who had escaped the enforced repatriation to Japan organised by the Americans in 1946, and who had stayed on in China as mercenaries. Finally, to my surprise, in many of the front-line Communist units at least a third of the soldiers were women.

There was a veritable cocktail of rifles strewn about, Japanese 'Arisaka' and British Lee-Enfield SMLE and a smattering of American M1 Garands. These all seemed discarded and had obviously been taken off Nationalist soldiers when they had surrendered. In contrast the Ba Lu Jun (Communists) seemed equipped with Garands, US M1Carbines and the occasional Thompson submachine gun. There were various varieties of Mausers of indeterminate origin and ownership littering the ground, generally with their external wooden holsters which doubled to extend the stock. All these rifles were of various calibres and varying cartridge lengths, which must have made provision of ammunition a logistical nightmare.

I was not paying much attention to where my feet went and suddenly I stepped on something that squashed under my tread. Bending down to pick it up, it looked like a rifle bullet. The brass cartridge case was intact but the bullet was flattened and appeared to be cardboard wrapped in copper foil. I called out to Dad and Mr Jeffery, the British Consul, and they came over, both of them very interested. Then the plot thickened, because Dad read the ammunition box from which the rounds had tumbled out, to discover that the rifle rounds had been made in Japan for export to the Chinese in 1927. Now, when Japan invaded Manchuria in 1931 and then swept down China after the July 1937 Marco Polo incident, the Japanese officers had briefed their infantry thus: 'The Chinese will shoot at you, but do not fear as the bullets will only bruise you.' That is certainly all that that these foil-cased cardboard rounds would have done at the time. And, twenty-two years later, even if the propellant had ignited I doubt if it would have caused even a bruise.

After a very educational and instructive two hours Dad decided that we had gone far enough forward, as the front was now only a quarter of a mile away and bullets were still flying about. It was time to retreat for home, and lunch was in order. Dad explained to Mum what we had seen; I am not sure she was certain that I really needed that sort of education. But the staff were still in the Hotel, the intermittent firing was still occurring, so Mum let matters stand.

The next morning two Communist officers arrived; they were quite relaxed about my parents, having seen their passports, and Roger, but took an extraordinary interest in me. I suspect now it was because I had on a pair of blue jeans and a navy blue sweater. Anyhow they asked me who I was and Dad confirmed that I was his son. That still did not satisfy them and I was asked – no, ordered – to accompany them to a small office room downstairs in the Hotel. As soon as the door was shut they rounded on me and accused me of being a US sailor. Something I vehemently denied. They then tried another approach, and all this was going on in Chinese. Then they started getting really nasty and, probably only for effect, fired a Luger through the ceiling, saying that the next bullet was for me unless I admitted that I was an American Naval rating. Realising that I had not made much impression on their obviously firm beliefs, I changed tack and said 'Comrades. I cannot admit to something that is not true. I am a student at St Louis College,' and produced my student badge from that establishment. I added: 'I am underage for a British passport and you will find that I am listed on my mother's.' The word student, *xue sheng*, seemed to mollify them and suddenly it was all smiles and the interview was over. It had taken nearly eight hours, and was not an experience that I was keen to repeat.

Ten days later we learnt that General Fu Zuoyi had surrendered a quarter of a million Nationalist soldiers at Beijing. Obviously, the price was right. The 'little' war was over and the victors could sweep south to the Yangtze River. But first they had to deal with the prisoners captured from the three regiments borrowed from Fu Zuoyi. Down the road from our flat at the back of the Court Hotel, on the lamp posts near the Gordon Hall, the victors were stringing up the vanquished. The prisoners' fate was a rope under the arms and round the back of the neck; then the hapless victims were suspended from the lamp posts, and ultimately their corpses were used for bayonet practice. The dead were cut down a week or so later. There was no smell of death as the temperature barely ever rose above zero.

16

The New Regime Arrives

Things slowly returned to the way they had been prior to the fighting. By mid-February the Red Duster had come down off the pole on the roof: it had served its purpose. By March, St Louis College started up again and it was a cycle to school each morning, home for lunch and back again until tea-time, now no shells as hazards, but the city was still littered with unexploded ordnance. The new regime did not interfere at all and suddenly there was no need whatsoever to grease officials' palms. Those civilian officials captured from the previous regime started being taken off in truckloads, with wooden neck placards telling the world the nature of their crimes. The trucks ended up on the west boundary of Tianjin, where the human contents were herded into groups. They no doubt were given the same treatment that I had witnessed in the village near Weihsien nearly four years before, but which now seemed like a century ago. A sight that was denied most 'Westerners' by the area being declared prohibited. However, once again my 'student badge' worked wonders with the semi-literate soldiery.

I had got friendly again with an American, Johnny Hoch, during the previous year. He was a year younger than I, although I had met him in Weihsien, and his father was a retired US Army Veterinary Surgeon who had married a Russian and settled in Tianjin. Once the fighting was over and it was safe to go out of the city, Johnny invited me to ride out to his father's dairy, about four miles north-east of Tianjin. This became a weekly occurrence, always travelling on our bicycles. I enjoyed being with the animals: there was a herd of cows, some horses and goats. These were survivors of an Aid Programme, the livestock having been sent out to China by the US Government for the people of China, post-war. Johnny's father, as a vet, had 'inherited the herd' because they had been so neglected by the Chinese city dwellers, both underfed and in pain from being under-milked. R. J. Hoch branched out as a dairyman, much to the delight of people like my parents, as safe undiluted fresh milk was now available. Delivery was easy. A cyclist with about 150 cotton pockets sewn round the bicycle frame to hold the bottles could do it, as traditional milk bottles were difficult to obtain. Customers were soon content with brown 'bourbon' bottles with a screw top.

In March 1949 the ride through the outskirts of the city to the farm was certainly 'educational', dodging near-wild dogs with human body parts in their jaws, or fighting over possession of a woman's leg, having dug out the bodies involuntarily buried by shellfire from the 60,000 reported killed during the siege and just after. The roads had been tarmacked long before, but the impact of artillery shells had left the surface erratic, and definitely in need of patching. The advancing year drove the temperature up, and the partially buried bodies just added to the smell, ever present in the air.

Tianjin had been surrounded by bandits or warring factions since the early 19th century, and it had never been really safe to go into the countryside without weapons, especially immediately before and after the Second World War. That was fine for Dad, when he went shooting duck or snipe, but the dangers had always prevented children from straying far outside the city. Now all that changed – I could wander round the countryside at will.

And in April I got out to the Hochs' farm and found it in crisis, as half of the herd had got bloat. Probably due to the very lush grass, which had been abundantly fertilised by human bodies. Doc Hoch welcomed me and asked me to help. He inspected all the cattle, some of which were in a bad way. After very brief instruction, I started using a trochar[77] and cannula, hammering the trochar into the suffering beasts' stomachs then pulling it out to release the pressure, which inevitably meant getting some of the 'mixture' over my clothes. Despite trying to clean myself up at the farm, when I got home I was accused by Mum of stinking. Which was probably true, because my sense of smell has never been very good, and I was quite oblivious to second-hand, partly digested grass. Brought up among the effluent of China, rotten smells never did make much of an impact on my nasal passages.

Just as things returned to apparent normality, news came on 17th May that HMS *Amythst* was stuck in the Yangtze near Nanking and had been shelled by Communist artillery; the story filled the radio and the English language press. Probably the same 155mm guns that had been used at Tianjin. The local rumour amongst the foreign community was that *Amythst*'s journey up the Yangtze was due to the British Embassy at Nanking having run out of gin. Which I could believe, as gin and tonic had built the East India

Company. If tonic was not available Angostura bitters would be, and a recourse could always be made to drinking 'Pink Gins', as adults were adamant that gin was essential to the wellbeing of the British stomach in the Far East. HMS *Amythst* finally escaped the Yangtze on 2nd June 1949.

The Americans had steadfastly backed Chiang Kai-shek and the Guomindang (Nationalists). Now that that former regime was out of favour, the American Consulate had to be closed and items disposed of. The US Information Services had endowed a large library, which had been shipped in under some other aid programme. This had to find a new home, and it was given to St Louis School. I was considered by Brother Kenny, the Headmaster, to be ahead of my class so I got the 'job' of supervising the transfer of the entire library to the school premises. I had rapidly to learn the Dewey system of decimal cataloguing, which was an intriguing job, and lasted to the end of term. This was inevitably extended because I often paused to read an 'interesting' article or book. Meanwhile I had really taken to softball, which of course I had played in Weihsien, the school yard being too small for proper baseball.

Summer holidays arrived suddenly. We would have to endure the heat of the city as it was not considered prudent to go to Beidaihe. Fortunately, the Country Club was now operating normally, as for the first two years after the Second World War it had been requisitioned as a US Officers Club by the USMC Third Amphibious Corps. The Club had not been considered safe when the US Marines left Tianjin as it was outside the main populated area of the city, and the refurbishment that had started in March 1948 had been rudely interrupted by the civil war. Membership rules were now more relaxed, as the number of Europeans had been decimated with people leaving before the civil-war fighting.

Also, the Cercle Francais Club had been requisitioned by the new Chinese Army. Thus it was decided to concentrate the leisure facilities in one venue. The re-opening of the Race Club was out of the question as there were neither horses nor jockeys.

Summer of 1949 was in a way idyllic: a little gentle school, lovely weather and an occasional trip in a punt. Come September it was back to St Louis. With the acquisition of the US Information Library, the school had abandoned the Cambridge Overseas School Certificate syllabus. In future, transitional procedures were in force and the school undertook to host the 1949 examinations. So I would study for the Cambridge Junior Examinations to be held in December 1949 under the school's auspices.

Christmas came and went. Freda and Tullis came round just after Christmas; they had had a quiet time since Granny Bridge had died in her sleep on 9th November 1949. She had been poorly most of the year and had been living with Aunt Freda in their house on Parkes Road, Tianjin for the past seven years.

As far as I was concerned the use of the Country Club swimming pool in the summer and the squash court in the winter was adequate. I was taught squash by and often played with Rev Archie Briggs, the High Church Anglican clergyman who had arrived as priest in charge at All Saints Church in 1947. These two 'indoor' sports, as well as softball in the summer and soccer in the colder months, was sufficient.

Matting sheds had been built in a large school off Race Course Road and the ground flooded so ice hockey was possible. I had a strange encounter in January 1950. I was playing ice hockey and fell skidding across the ice, until my journey was brought to a halt by the 'telegraph' pole that supported the matting roof. There was a girl who had been figure skating round the periphery who was now resting against the cross-bar, about three feet above the ice. I hit the post with such force with my thigh that I spun around and knocked her legs from under her and she sat down on top of me. How I did not break my leg I do not know, especially when the bruise came out from knee to hip. After the apologies I found that her name was Marga Meinert, and that she was a St Joseph's pupil, but not a close friend of the sisters of my own friends from St Louis. Something clicked when we were lying on the ice, and I knew my parents would not object as she was pure Caucasian. Marga and her great friend Monica Wolff, as chaperone, were then recruited into our walks, picnics and jaunts around the countryside of Tianjin. During the winter months the ground was frozen enough but come summer there was a problem, in that there was a lot of water and one needed a boat. Very soon a trade hiring out flat-bottomed sampans grew up. Based on the water around the Country Club, a day's picnicking was on the agenda most weekends, whether school was on or not. Johnny had a sister of my age, Hazel, and so we were able to gather together a good half-dozen friends to have a day out in what was in effect a large punt. The boys, mainly Russian, were known to Johnny's mother, and the girls mainly Hazel's friends; my brother was still too young to be involved.

1950 bubbled along in this vein. St Louis had a sports day in early May and then it was softball. There was an interruption late May when an enormous explosion sounded from down-river at the Arsenal. The windows of the flat that had survived the city's bombardment eighteen months before were blown out. It turned out that Nationalist POWs were moving bombs and ammunition, and some had gone off, though whether by accident or design I never found out.

In July, the countryside being completely in the hands of the Communists, it was deemed safe enough to travel by train, so the Bridge family reverted to its long-held habits and three weeks were spent at the Beidaihe property. It was not really the same, anymore. The last visit had been in 1948, when the euphoria of post-war hopes was at its highest, but now came the realisation that the world had changed. Previously there had always been a lot of the family present, and I could catch up with my cousins. In 1950 I had to content myself in small boats, the familiar smell of sun-dried fish in the scuppers. Sadly Roger was too young to participate and my contemporaries were still all in Tianjin, so I was on my own to amuse myself.

Mid-August it was back to Tianjin. We learnt by letter that my Uncle Harold was still trying to get a visa to enter China and relieve Dad so that I could be taken back to England to finish school. Mum felt that the family unit should stay together. Communications with the outside world were fairly erratic again. Time was marching on, and then it was established that the St Louis syllabus was going to firmly follow the curriculum of the Catholic University of Washington DC, USA. I realised that it was going to have to be another 'do it yourself' job, like the previous year's Junior School Certificate had been. I told Mum that she was going to have to organise the papers for me to sit, and find somewhere for me to sit them with acceptable invigilation. For studying French I could piggyback on St Louis, because the language was a lost cause anyway. I knew a fair bit of Geography, Mathematics, Physics and Chemistry and there were sufficient reference books around. English Literature, with its nominated books, was another matter. Teaching for the American exam had been very different, so short of learning all the nominated books on the Cambridge syllabus verbatim (and even then risking missing the nuances that the Examination Board would put on the papers) I decided that it was best avoided, and I should concentrate on my better subjects.

My mother had, by invitation, taken up the post of the British Consul-General's office manager in March 1949, soon after the Communists had taken over the Government. This was partially for security considerations. Keeping the Consular staff British-born ensured that there could be no blackmailing of even minor officials. Mum had worked for the Tianjin Branch of the Chartered Bank in the late 1920s, thus she had the shorthand and typing skills and office procedures as a background, and it did not take her long to hone them into Whitehall procedures. She went to see the Consul-General one day in September 1950 and came home to say that my examinations were all sorted. When I queried this she said that Mr Jeffery had agreed to his office being used as an examination room, and he would do the invigilating. The University had agreed to send the examination papers to a Hong Kong address, and the completed examination papers would be returned to Cambridge with the HK-completed examination papers. I could see a hole in this arrangement: as I was in Tianjin, how were the papers to cover that 1,500 miles to and from Hong Kong? Before I could point this out, Mum added that she had got permission for the papers to be addressed to the Consul-General and for the King's Messenger to carry the papers to and from Hong Kong in the Diplomatic Mail Bag. Although the logistics were sorted, I would still have to 'cram' if I were to hold any hope of passing.

In October Uncle Tullis and Aunt Freda stayed at the Court for a few days, before sailing on Jardine Matheson's SS *Toksang* on 13th October. Uncle Harold and Aunt Hilda were staying at the Court, so the two brothers and their eldest sister all met for the last time together.

The rest of the year disappeared into a frenzy of activity, but by mid-December the exam was over and I was ready to start ice hockey, though first Christmas intervened. I had been induced to join the St Louis School choir some months ago. I am certain that it was due to my clarity of diction: it certainly could not be from my musical ability, but then again why should clarity in English have been such a factor, when most of the action was in Latin plainsong? I did grow to like it, and nearly seventy years on I am still addicted to it. Midnight Mass at St Louis Church was moving. So was the walk home, trying to get through a solid line of battalions of marching soldiery off to reinforce the North Koreans in the Korean War. The next day among my Christmas presents was a book, *Mutiny on the Bounty*, by Nordhoff and Hall. It had obviously stayed on the bookshop's racks since it had been printed in 1936. I read it with great interest. But looking back I recall the coloured illustrations: one in particular was of Fletcher Christian at Tubuai on Rarotonga Island. I said to myself: 'I am going to get there some day.'[78]

On Boxing Day I went on an expedition to the southwest of Tianjin with half a dozen others, all on skates as the streams and ponds were well frozen. I learnt the hard way that it was foolhardy to try and skate downstream of a Chinese village. Initially it was all right; then came an ominous cracking sound and the ice started breaking up. I threw myself at the bank but not before getting thoroughly wet, almost to the waist. There was nothing for it but to wait for my jeans to dry on me whilst I skated home. Needless to say, when I did get home the jeans rapidly thawed in the central heating, and the stench of the village water filled the air. Once again I was in for an admonishment from Mum,

'Where is that smell coming from?' I had to admit that was not the first occasion I had come home with the aroma of effluent, but pointed out to Mum that at least it came from a variety of sources: a cesspit, a cow's guts and now a village sewer.

Now the die was cast: assuming that I got an exit visa I could go back to the UK. As the Cambridge examination results would not be 'out' until the beginning of April, May seemed eminently suitable. But first to get a job. Being a little naïve I did not think that I was really suited to a nine-to-five office job, and indicated that exploiting my 'bent' for chemistry might be an idea. Dad seized upon this and wrote to one of the directors of ICI[79] in London. Back came the reply that he would be delighted to see me in May when I got back to the UK. So that seemed the future almost settled; I just hoped that it would work out as meticulously planned.

On my 17th birthday I had a party in the flat. Mum was a bit apprehensive of the people on the guestlist: people whose parents she knew, however tenuously, got the tick of approval immediately; others she accepted. There were only about eighteen people, all around my age. I had invited Marga and Monica because I knew the former would not come without the latter. The evening was worth it, as I got a deep kiss from the former, for which I had been angling for some time. I was not to know it then, but we did keep in touch and corresponded for the next six years before circumstances prevented us getting any closer.

April Fool's Day I got my Cambridge results: English Language, Geography, Additional Mathematics, Physics and Chemistry all Credits, and Elementary Mathematics Very Good, whereas French was just a Pass. No matter: under the published rules it meant that I could apply to London University for a 'Matriculation Exemption'. This

I did, posting the letter to London and requesting that the reply be sent to my Uncle Alwyne's address in Surrey.

My last day at St Louis was 26th April, and then school athletics on Saturday 5th May. As usual one was expected to try and compete in the whole range. I fell badly on the high jump, clearing six feet. My left elbow was very painful, but I did not think much of it.

My parents had been deeply into amateur dramatics since before they were married. The 'expatriate' Tianjin Amateur Dramatics Society had been in existence since before the Boxer Rebellion. They were putting on Noël Coward's *Blithe Spirit*, and I had been roped in to do the electrics. The venue was the Country Club and the live performances scheduled for the 2nd and 4th of May.

Then on 8th May the authorities telephoned to say that my 'exit visa' was approved, and so I went round to collect it before anybody changed their minds. By the 10th my elbow was still seriously swollen, so Mum rang up Dr Grice. The Friday dawned with weather perfect and I went down Chieh Fang Pei Lu to the doctor's surgery, which was only in the next block. An immediate X-ray was thought necessary and I was asked to go to the British Hospital, about two miles distant, straight away.

There was a problem, as about a quarter of a million Chinese were milling round the streets: 'Rent-a-Crowd' for support of the Chinese Army in Korea. I could see that to get anywhere drastic action was necessary. With my arm in a sling I walked to the nearest Military Police post. I explained to the Lieutenant that I had damaged my elbow at sports and the doctor had said that it must be X-rayed, and could he help me get to the hospital. I showed my St Louis student badge and within five minutes I was being driven in his Jeep to the hospital.

A sling to support the arm for a month was all that was prescribed. The bonus was that the driver had been instructed to wait for me. And so I was driven home, returning to an interrogation from Mum about just where I had been. It turned out that someone had seen me driving off in the Chinese Army Jeep and had telephoned Mum, who had jumped to the conclusion that I had been arrested. I just asked her why she hadn't rung the hospital, as they would have told her I was safely in the X-ray Department!

17

The Journey to England

The next week was packing to leave China, and I got most things into two Revelation suitcases. On May 19th 1951 I embarked on the SS *Hunan* at 5 p.m., and found that I was sharing a cabin with Ray Sayers of HSBC,[80] who had been relieved as the local manager after serving in Tianjin for two and a half years. Mum and Dad came on board for an hour or so at 7 p.m. That was the last time I saw Dad.[81] The next day at 7.30 a.m. the SS *Hunan* sailed. Winding down the Hai Ho, the countryside looked little changed, although there was evidence of factories springing up near Dagu, but across the river Danggu looked desolate. After crossing the bar the pilot disembarked and the open sea beckoned. It was a gentle swell and the only motion the forward passage of the ship. We could see the hills of the Shandong Peninsula as we hugged the coast. From there it was almost due south.

There was occasional aircraft activity. The Korean War was in full swing and reconnaissance aircraft were everywhere, mostly USAF land-based ones, but also the occasional RAF Sunderland flying boat could be seen. The SS *Hunan*'s forward hatch had an enormous Union Jack painted on it to confirm our identity. The ship's course slowly turned south-west as we paralleled to the coast of China. We docked at Kowloon early on the morning of May 28ᵗʰ 1951. Mum's friend Mrs Hilda Hale was there to meet me.

The Hales lived not far from the wharf on Chatham Road. Mum had arranged that I stay with them during my brief visit to Hong Kong. My parents met the Hales when he had been manager of Thomas Cook's Travel Service in Beijing many years before, and I knew their daughters from Weihsien days, where they had lived in adjacent blocks. Hilary was two years my junior and Beryl then a girl of eleven. During the ten days I was staying with the Hales I got taken to the statutory sights of Hong Kong. The second morning I was there I got a phone call, as I was warned by Mum that I would. A very 'correct' voice said that they would pick me up the next evening and take me out to the Hong Kong Hotel on the Island. I felt that I must tell my hosts, and permission was granted. I was duly picked up and a very intense conversation was held throughout the evening, and I was dropped back at the Hales at about eleven. My hosts for the evening might just as well have been dressed in Burberrys and trilby hats, but the things that I had seen cycling through the streets of Tianjin, and the places in the city to which my St Louis student badge had gained me access, were of obvious interest. Over the previous six months Tianjin had been the marshalling point for the Chinese Army en route to help the North Koreans in their war against the American-led United Nations forces.

Almost too quickly it was time to move on. On 8ᵗʰ June Mrs Hale took me to the P&O ship RMS *Carthage*,[82] moored at the same Kowloon pier where I had arrived, and she saw me to my cabin. It was tourist class at the rear of the ship, and I estimated near the waterline. I suspected that when we got underway I would feel the vibration of the propellers. There seemed to be a lot of Scouts milling about, and I learnt that it was the Hong Kong Contingent off to the World Scout Jamboree, which was being held in Austria in July. I had heard about this latter as Dad was very interested in Scouting and had been the Assistant Commissioner for North China before the war.

The cabin was for four males, and my fellow travellers, I established, were a near sixty-year-old Greek who kept himself to himself; 'Jock', a Scots policeman who was going back to Scotland having served two years with the HK Police; and Tim, a Lance Bombardier of the Royal Artillery going on leave to visit his parents in Bombay (Mumbai).

The journey to Singapore was uneventful, and we docked there early on 12th June. Then there was only half a day to go ashore, time for a brief taxi drive round the centre for four of us, three from my cabin and 'Digger', an Australian who had served in the Australian Army in New Guinea during the Second World War. Digger was going to the UK on a posting from Lever Brothers and was in an adjacent cabin. Then back to the ship for lunch. The next stop was Penang, where we moored alongside the pier not far from Fort Cornwallis. We docked early and learnt that we had all day ashore as there was a lot of cargo to load.

We wandered round the mosque area and then had a look at the Chinese quarter. The smell of food was more Chinese than I remembered from China itself. We then decided to go up the funicular railway to the top of Penang Hill, which was 2,600 feet. Penang was itself an enigma: the city itself was called Georgetown, and sat largely within the confines of Fort Cornwallis, a Napoleonic-era fort, which the British had acquired as part of the colony of the Straits Settlements in 1826. It was ceded to what would become Malaysia in 1947. The population is mainly Hokkien Chinese and Indians from the Coromandel coast.

Having got up to the top of the hill we walked down the path alongside the railway, getting back for tea on the *Carthage*. The ship sailed at 8 and soon it was due west until we reached the island of Sri Lanka.[83] Mooring in the harbour we got ashore by tender, and as before there was only half a day. Then it was a relatively short journey up the west coast of India to Bombay where we anchored up in the Roads and were ferried to the wharf, which had an enormous arch: 'The Gateway to India'. Tim's parents were there to meet him. They had settled in India after the father was demobbed from the British Army. They were very hospitable and quickly asked all four of us to lunch. Their flat was in a block not far from the Victoria Terminus, the huge railway station. I could not refuse. So we meandered along the streets of Bombay and eventually reached their flat. The cold beer was very welcome. Then lunch was served, and to my dismay it was curry. I managed to eat some and I hope I did not show that curry was usually too spicy for me. But it tasted better than expected.

Now we were down to three, and the journey to Aden was uneventful. The *Carthage* arrived at Aden in the morning, and as we were moored in the 'Roads' it seemed sensible to delay a trip ashore until after lunch. This the three of us did. Steamer Point was surrounded by grey gaunt hills. There was a 'D' shaped pattern of streets, filled mostly by the shops of Indian traders. There was a small hotel called the 'Rock' which, like the rest of Steamer Point, seemed a little tired and decrepit.

Four days north up the Red Sea to Suez. A brief stop at the entrance to the Canal and then a night passage to Port Said.

It was quite intriguing how a huge 'battery-box', complete with a very bright searchlight, was hoisted at the bows of the ship to enable the pilot to see his way along. Mooring at Port Said, there was not much to see ashore. The 'bum boats' and 'gully-gully men'[84] on the other side of the ship from the shore kept us entertained with diving for coins and trying to trade using thin ropes thrown over the railings, on which one could hoist articles up, sending the payment down by the same method.

Sailed from Port Said on the afternoon of the 1st July, and three days later it was the coast of Tunisia and then Algeria. Heading west we went through the Straits of Gibraltar at night but woke up with the Spanish coast on the starboard side and the Atlantic Ocean surprisingly calm.

We made a brief stop at Brixham to pick up the Channel pilot and now we sailed east-north-east to go up the Channel. Dawn found us in the Thames Estuary heading west to Tilbury, where we moored mid-morning.

England, at last, on 11th July 1951.

Immigration was quick and with none of the convolutions the family had experienced arriving in Liverpool back in 1946. I was given ration tickets for two weeks. I don't know whether the address that I had given – I was going to stay for two weeks with my uncle Sir Alwyne Ogden and his wife Lady Jessie, Dad's older sister – sped the process. My passport was stamped and I was told go to the Farnham Registration Office by the end of July to get a permanent ration card.

I went to Waterloo Station and then took the train to Farnham, Surrey, which I reached about tea-time. Uncle Alwyne was there to meet me. When I got to Wickham House Aunt Jessie handed me my mail. An official one from London University enclosing a rejection of my application for Matriculation, as the scheme had closed on 31st March 1951 and they could not accept late applications. Having thought about this I decided it was unfair, as I had in fact acted as soon as I could, given the circumstances. I felt that a personal plea might be the most effective method, because I wanted that Matric Certificate in my hand when I saw ICI.

A week later I caught the Greenline Bus and in just over an hour found myself at Senate House, London University. Went up to the receptionist and asked for the author of the letter by name. I said that I did not have an appointment but had come up from Farnham and would be grateful if he could see me, as there appeared a misunderstanding in his letter to me. Time was not a problem to me and I would wait until he was available. After an hour the receptionist, seeing that I was content to stick it out, decided suddenly that a short meeting was possible and I was invited in. I thanked him for seeing me at short notice and explained that I had sat the examination in the Consul-General's office in Tianjin, which was behind the Bamboo Curtain, last December.

The Consulate, not being an educational establishment, had been unable to furnish me with the cut-off date. I had acted with all speed when I got the result, which, I now found out, happened to fall a week *after* the deadline. It would appear that arbitrary bureaucracy was going to blight my future by not allowing my educational achievements, such as they were to date, to be recognised. In the light of this evidence, I said that I would appreciate it were the University to reconsider the decision.

The Secretary heard me in silence, but he seemed to grasp the situation. Two days later, with a brief covering letter, I duly received my Matriculation Certificate, dated 31st March 1951.

Then I had my appointment with the ICI Director, and I duly turned up at their office in Millbank, London. A very pleasant coffee and chat ensued, in which I said that I would hope they could find me a place in their medicine or paints division, as I felt that my forte was chemicals. The next week I found that I had been allocated to the Lime Division in Buxton Derbyshire, which was expanding. I was to start my first job on 1st September 1951, in just over a month's time, and ICI would arrange accommodation in Buxton.

With his letter in my pocket I set off for Mirfield on 1st August to stay with my second cousins.

Epilogue

After a very enjoyable month in Mirfield, I duly reported to ICI Lime Division in Buxton on 31st August 1951. I had been booked into a bed and breakfast, out towards Lightwood Reservoir. And I started work as a laboratory assistant in the laboratories situated in Dove Dale. I rapidly realised that a degree was necessary if I were going to get anywhere. Derbyshire County Council's education department had different ideas and latched onto the notion that, as my parents were not ratepayers and lived abroad, they could not sponsor me. This went on until the University term started. Then the issue of National Service came up, with no actual starting date proposed, and in any case my liability was subject to debate as I had been in a Japanese camp. I could see no future as a permanent lab assistant. So, one evening, I walked into Manchester's RAF recruiting shop and asked to join the RAF as aircrew, which I did on the 3rd March 1952, my eighteenth birthday. The delay occasioned because I could not get written parental permission, my parents still being in Communist China. I also felt that I must give ICI the contracted three months' notice, but cited National Service as the reason.

I was commissioned into the RAF on 16th June 1952 and

commenced flying training shortly after. By April 1954 I was on my first operational tour with 216 Squadron in the Suez Canal Zone, Egypt. Subsequent postings took me to serve on UK-based transport squadrons, but flying all over the world. Visits to the H-bomb site on Christmas Island (now Kiritimati) culminated in a very pleasant year there flying Dakota aircraft in the South Pacific. Then it was to Singapore in early 1959, where I met a WRAF Signals Officer and we were married late that year in England. By this time I held a permanent commission in the RAF. 1962 saw the birth of our first child and the start of a three-year posting to the Royal Canadian Air Force, flying to and fro across the Atlantic, from which I returned to Transport Command, where I was awarded the Air Force Cross.

In 1971 I could see the retraction into Fortress Britain, and decided to exercise an option and retire from the RAF. The future was uncertain and we now had three coming four children, but I was convinced something would turn up. Entering civil aviation at London Gatwick I flew for Dan Air Ltd, before being offered a post to introduce the Boeing 707 into a charter airline, British Airtours, being formed by the state-owned British European Airways. I was joining part of the flight operations management, where I stayed until the merger of British Airways with British Caledonian, when I was promoted to Senior Manager, British Airways at London Heathrow. Shortly after I was given the additional responsibilities of Flight Operations Director of a partially owned subsidiary, GB Airways, a Boeing 737 and Airbus A320 European operator. The Executive Directorship followed for three years, when I retired from full-time employment, continuing with consultancy for four years. I had been elected to Fellowships of the Royal Institute of Navigation and the Royal Aeronautical Society.

On entering civil aviation I accepted the Freedom of the Honourable Company of Air Pilots, a London Livery Company. This was followed by the Freedom of the City of London, and then I was elected Master of the Company in 1997.

As an aside from aviation I was elected to the Committee of the Chairmanship of the Association of British Civilian Internees of the Far East Region. Although I was not affected personally, I was appalled when the Ministry of Defence decided, when implementing an edict from then Prime Minister Tony Blair, that British passport-holders who were interned by Japan were *not* British if they were born Jewish, were coloured, were born in Ireland or were women who had obtained British nationality by marriage prior to 1941. Hence these categories could not get what was called an 'ex-gratia' payment of £10,000. Through ABCIFER's solicitors I managed to get four QCs to act *pro bono*. And defeat the MoD in the High Court, ably supported by 300 Members of Parliament. I was appointed an MBE in 2007.

Now, surrounded my mother's diaries of the 1940s and my memories of Weihsien, Beidaihe and Tianjin, writing in Sussex, I realise that I should have put my experiences on paper half a century ago.

Endnotes

1   All Chinese place names are in the current Pinyin spelling. Tianjin (Pinyin) was written as Tientsin (Wade Giles) up until 1949, although it was sometimes written as Tiensing in the 19th century. The present Pinyin has always been the pronunciation and means 'Heaven's (or Sky's) Ford'.

2   Treaty Ports were of three types:

    1. Ports near the coast with a Chinese Maritime Customs Office were open to foreign commerce.

    2. Settlements were a designated district under the control of a Foreign Consul.

    3. Concessions were *de jure* colonies of the country, leasing the property with the Foreign Consul having legal and political authority over the Concession(s) and whilst Chinese and nationals of other countries could reside, the controlling Consul could exclude entry into the territory.

3   The Treaty of Nanking 29th August 1842 (UKNA FO682/1976/92) identified five Treaty Ports – Canton, Amoy, Foochow, Ningpo and Shanghai. There was a subsidiary Treaty in 1843 and an exchange of Letters of Understanding in 1844. Hong Kong was ceded in 1841 as a result of that war.

4   Dagu known up until 1949 as Taku and on the other side of the river Tungku (Wade Giles).

5   Beijing was adopted as the spelling from 1958. Until then the city was known by various names, including Peiping, Pekin or Peking (Wade Giles), meaning Northern Capital.

6   Larger vessels offloaded on to 'lighters' which were then towed up to Tianjin by tugs.

7   *The Treaty Ports of China and Japan*, Mayers, Dennys, King Trubner & Co. London 1867.

8   Treaty of Tianjin (Tientsin) 1858 – UKNA FO 881/1569(in English) FO1080/346 and FO1080/360 (in the original Chinese).

9   Marriage Register (Pontypridd 11a 524)

10   P&O Line launched in 1880.

11   The Imperial Canal built in the 4th century BC between Beijing and Hangzhou, the Yangtse.

12   'China's Millions', *Journal of the China Inland Mission* 1892.

13   LMS Archives in SOAS.

14   London Missionary Society Register of Missionaries 1896-1923 entry 1104 (SOAS).

15   Flat-bottomed coastal sailing boat.

16   Always the Chinese name but known as Chefoo by Europeans during the late 19th and 20th centuries.

17   Tsysi taiheo (1835–1908) the adoptive mother of Tetsung (who reigned as Emperor Guangxu 1875–1908).

18   Letter, Hopkin Rees to LMS, London 9th January 1903 (SOAS).

19   A. H. Bridge was the ultimate Chinese interpreter at the British Court in Shanghai.

20   Taipans were the owners and managing directors of businesses.

21   Meeston Batchelor writing in *Cradle of Empire* 1981.

22   The 'Carrot' to the latter was that they could apply for British passports after 5 years' service.

23   Bund was a continuous wharf or bank on the sides of a river.

24   A Chinese gambling game played with 144 pieces or tiles.

25   W. H. Cogland political resident Aden, quoted in *Elixir of Empire*, P. J. Rich 1989.

26   7th July 1937 – *Encyclopaedia Britannica*.

27   A China coast innovation was the 'Noble Order of British Spitfires' where members were encouraged to raise money and the amount recognised by advancing up the rank structure of the Royal Air Force.

28   Amah or a slight variation was the generic name of a child's nurse throughout the Far East.

29   My amah employed by my mother to child-mind me.

30   *British and Indian Armies on the China Coast*, Alan Harfield.

31   Britain had always used police from another part of the Commonwealth. The White Russians evicted by Communism were keen candidates as after 5 years they were eligible for British passports, whereas others had a 10-year residency requirement.

32   The 1st East Surrey Regiment got as far as Singapore where they surrendered on 15th February 1942 and spent the war years as POWs of Japan.

33   Le Rougetel, Counsellor British Embassy Shanghai Telegram 867 on 22nd September 1941 to Foreign Office London (FO 369/2676).

34   ibid.

35   Then Calcutta.

36   Special Operations Executive – of which Force 136 was its Far East Operation.

37   48 years later we both served as Vice Presidents of the Royal Institute of Navigation.

38   The British Concession kept English Bank Holidays.

39   The full Chinese characters for England were 'Ying Guo' or Ying Country.

40 A. G. N. Ogden and family left China on the *Kamakura Maru*. The former to become the British Consul-General in Kunming for the duration of the war, his wife to England. Ann to the WRNS in Ceylon and Brian commissioned into the Indian Army and then serving on Force 136 in Burma and Hanoi.

41 North China temperature varied from +33°C to -20°C during course of a year.

42 UKNA FO 371/31746, FO 371/35938, and IOR PJ/8/402.

43 His grand-son was Yul Brynner, a Hollywood actor in the 1960s.

44 The Swiss Consulate took over the maintenance of British Consular Births Marriages and Deaths Registers in addition to looking after the more usual interests.

45 Letter Ohta to Joerg dated 12th March 1943.

46 Located in the modern city of Weifang, Shandong, China.

47 Weifang on modern maps.

48 The Japanese allowed the chronically sick and those over 75 years to remain in their houses subject to the usual curfew, probably because they were one fewer mouth to feed.

49 The old Wade Giles name was Tsingtao.

50 Built 1924.

51 The abolition of the Emperors and the founding of the Republic.

52 Chinese food carriers were four metal dishes which fitted on top of each other with a lid held together with an external handle.

53 This story first appeared in *Bamboo Wireless* in June 2006 and then in the *Daily Mail* magazine on 16th May 2009.

54 Abbotsholme, an English public school in Derbyshire.

55 The town always known by Chinese as Yantai. I will use

Chefoo throughout this book for the school.

56   By carbon monoxide poisoning.

57   As an aside, Brian joined the Royal Navy and ended up as British Airways Concorde Technical Manager. Peter joined the RAF on National Service and was killed in a flying accident with the HK Auxiliary Air Force, and I spent 20 years in the RAF then a little longer with British Airways.

58   A tray of set gelatine on which non-drying ink is used on the original and copies are made by pressing down plain paper.

59   The parcel contained a tin of dried milk, (1lb) Spam, or corned beef, fruit biscuits, butter, 2oz Nescafe, bar of chocolate and raisins or prunes and a packet of US cigarettes.

60   Tiffin, a term first used in India, was the universal English name for lunch in the Far East.

61   Supper was the left-overs from tiffin. Dinner a more formal meal.

62   A senior NCO of the new guard.

63   Suicide.

64   A former American Presbyterian Mission College.

65   Spam was a processed pork loaf.

66   Similar to but more martial than Judo.

67   A nickname of a guard Sergeant who always used these words when he was spoken to. It meant 'Not allowed' in Chinese.

68   Courtesy of the US Red Cross.

69   Lt Moore had wangled his way on to the team as he had been a Chefoo schoolboy until 1939.

70   Report on Duck Mission by Major S. Staiger OSS China Theatre.

71   B25, a twin-engine aircraft bomber often used for

communication flights with the bomb doors bolted shut and wicker chairs fitted in the bomb-bay.

72 The United Nations Relief and Rehabilitation Administration (UNRRA).

73 Landing Ship Tank: a 4000-ton craft with a large bow doors and a well for tanks covered by a deck.

74 UNRRA.

75 Similar to the German Model 43 Stielhandgranat.

76 Chieh Fang Pei Lu.

77 The trochar was a spike-like surgical tool with a cannula tube. The latter left in to drain the stomach.

78 The author, by then an RAF Officer flying a C47, first visited Rarotonga in November 1958, just under eight years after reading the book in Communist China.

79 ICI: Imperial Chemical Industries, based in London but with a very strong presence in the Far East.

80 Ray went on to be Chairman of the Bank forty years later.

81 Albert Lionel Bridge died suddenly in Hong Kong on 30th August 1954 (aged fifty), after the time covered by this book.

82 One of P&O's 'Sisters': the RMS *Carthage*, *Canton* and *Corfu* on the Far East run from Tilbury between 1932 and 1951, except for WWII, each of 14,000 tonnes.

83 Then known as Ceylon.

84 Conjurers.

.